A LATERAL VIEW
essays on contemporary
JAPAN

A LATERAL VIEW
essays on contemporary
JAPAN

Donald Richie

The Japan Times, Ltd.
Tokyo, Japan
1987

For
Jean and Ted

ISBN 4-7890-0365-5

Published in Japan by the Japan Times, Ltd.

This book and many other fine books on Japan and the Japanese culture and language are published by and for the Japan Times, Ltd. located at 4-5-4 Shibaura, Minato-ku, Tokyo 108, Japan.

PRINTED IN JAPAN

Contents

Japan: A Description originally appeared in *Travel and Leisure*, reprinted in the *San Francisco Examiner*. *Japanese Shapes* originally, *Katachi, Japanese Patterns and Designs*, and *Design and Craftsmanship in Japan*, Tokyo Bijutsu Shuppan-sha/Abrams, Inc. *Japanese Rhythms*, originally in *East-West*, reprinted in the *Japan Society Newsletter*.

Tokyo, the Impermanent Capital, originally appeared in *Winds*, collected in *Some Aspects of Japanese Popular Culture*, Shubun, Int. *The 'Real' Disneyland*, originally, the *Japan Society Newsletter* as *Tokyo — the Real Disneyland*. *The City Home*, originally, the *Japan Society Newsletter*. *Walking in Tokyo*, originally appeared in *Tokyo: Form and Spirit*. Walker Art Center/Abrahms, reprinted in *Japan Society Newsletter*.

Gesture as Language originally appeared in *Some Aspects of Japanese Popular Culture*, Shubun, Int. *Signs and Symbols* appeared in *Ji: Signs and Symbols of Japan*, Kodansha Int., Ltd. *A Vocabulary of Taste* originally appeared in *House and Garden*. *The Tongue of Fashion* originally appeared in *Some Aspects of Japanese Popular Culture*, Shubun, Int., reprinted, the *Japan Society Newsletter* as *The Language of Fashion*.

Notes on the Noh appeared in *The Hudson Review*. *Kyogen* appeared in *The Oriental Economist*, reprinted in *A Guide to Kyogen*, Hinoki Shoten. *Japan's Avantgarde Theatre* appeared in the *Japan Foundation Newsletter*. *The Strata of Japanese Drama* originally appeared in the *Japan Society Newsletter*.

Women in Japanese Cinema, *British Film Institute Bulletin*, variously reprinted. *The Japanese Eroduction* originally published in *Film Comment*, reprinted, *Some Aspects of Japanese Popular Culture*, Shubun, Int. *A Definition of the Japanese Film*, originally published in *Performance*, reprinted, Shubun, Int., as above.

Japanese TV: The Presentational Image, originally published in *Some Aspects of Japanese Popular Culture*, Shubun, Int. *Pachinko* originally published in *Winds*, reprinted, Shubun, Int., as above. *Mizushobai: The Art of Pleasing* originally appeared in the *Japan Society Newsletter*. *The Japanese Kiss* originally appeared in *Winds*. *Walkman, Manga and Society* originally appeared in the Japan Society Newsletter.

All the essays are here republished with permission.

Introduction

THESE ESSAYS cover a period of nearly fifteen years. The earliest was written in 1962 and the latest appeared last year, in 1986. All have been published elsewhere, often republished as well, but this is the first collection to bring them all together.

I have divided these twenty-three essays into six sections. The first is about the country in general — descriptions of its shapes, patterns, rhythms. The second is about its capital, Tokyo. In the third, various "languages," are considered, not only Japanese itself but also the languages of gesture and of fashion. The fourth section is devoted to the drama of Japan, and the fifth to its cinema. Finally, the sixth section is about further popular culture — Japanese TV, *pachinko,* etc.

The date of each essay is given at its conclusion but I have also taken advantage of this opportunity to bring some of them up to date. In addition I have shortened several to avoid repeating information.

Donald Richie
1987

I

Japan: A Description

JAPAN IS ENTERED; the event is marked, as when one enters a Shinto shrine by passing beneath the *torii* gateway. There is an outside; then, there is an inside. And once inside — inside the shrine, inside Japan — the experience begins with a new awareness, a way of looking, a way of seeing.

You must truly observe. Go to the garden and look at the rock, the tree. Ah, nature, you say and turn — then stop. You have just observed that rock and tree have been placed there, placed by the hand of man, the Japanese hand. A new thought occurs: Nature does not happen; it is wrought. A new rule offers itself: Nothing is natural until it has been so created.

This comes as a surprise to us of a different culture. The Japanese view is anthropomorphic, unashamedly, triumphantly so. The gods here are human, and their mysteries are on display. If we occasionally find the Japanese scene mysterious, it is only because we find such simplicity mysterious — in the West, cause and effect this clear tend to be invisible. Look again at the torii — the support, the supported, and that is all.

Observation, appreciation and, through these, understanding. Not only in Japan, of course, but everywhere, naturally. But in Japan the invitation to observe is strongest because the apparent is so plain.

Look at the architecture. The floor defines the space; from it the pillars hold the beams; on them the roof contains the whole. Nothing is hidden. Traditionally there is no façade. Take the shrines at Ise. Cut wood, sedge, air — that is all they are made of.

The spatial simplicity extends temporally as well. The shrines have been destroyed and identically rebuilt every 20 years since antiquity. This cycle is an alternative to the Pyramids — a simpler answer to the claims of immortality. Rebuild precisely, and time is obliterated. Ise embodies the recipe for infinity: 100 cubits and two decades. That is all. Such simplicity, such economy suggest the metaphysical: The ostensible is the actual, the apparent is the real. We see what is there, and behind it we glimpse a principle.

Universal principles make up nature, but nature does not reveal these principles, in Japan, until one has observed nature by shaping it oneself. The garden is not natural until everything in it has been shifted. And flowers are not natural either until so arranged to be. God, man, earth — these are the traditional strata in the flower arrangement, but it is man that is operative, acting as the medium through which earth and heaven meet.

And the arrangement is not only in the branches, the leaves, the flowers. It is also in the spaces in between. Negative space is calculated, too — in the architecture, in the gardens, in the etiquette, in the language itself. The Japanese observes the spaces in between the branches, the pillars; he knows too when to leave out pronouns and when to be silent. Negative space has its own weight, and it is through knowing both negative and positive (yin and yang), the specific gravity of each, that one may understand the completed whole, that seamless garment that is life. There are, one sees, no opposites. The ancient Greek Heraclitus knew this, but we in the Western world forgot and are only now remembering. Asia never forgot; Japan always remembered.

If there are no true opposites, then man and nature are properly a part of one another. Seen from the garden, the house is another section of the landscape. The traditional roof is sedge, the stuff that flourishes in the fields. The house itself is wood, and the mats are reed — the outside brought inside.

The garden is an extension of the house. The grove outside is an extension of the flower arrangement in the alcove. Even now, when land prices make private gardens rare, the impulse continues. The pocket of earth outside the door contains a hand-reared tree, a flowering bush. Or, if that too is impossible, then the alcove in the single matted room contains a tiny tree, a flowering branch, a solitary bloom. Even now that sedge and reed are rarely used, the shapes they took continue — the Japanese reticulation of space insists on inside, outside, man-made nature made a part of nature, a continuing symbiosis. Even now, the ideal is that the opposites are one.

A garden is not a wilderness. It is only the romantics who find wildness beautiful, and the Japanese are too pragmatic to be romantic. At the same time, a garden is not a geometrical abstraction. It is only the classicists who would find that attractive, and the Japanese are too much creatures of their feelings to be so cerebrally classic. Rather, then, a garden is created to reveal nature. Raw nature is simply never there.

Paradigm: In Japan, at the old-fashioned inn, you get up, go to take your morning bath, and you are invisible — no one greets you. Only when you are dressed, combed, ready — only then comes the morning greeting. Unkempt nature, unkempt you, both are equally nonexistent. The garden prepared is acknowledged as natural. What was invisible is now revealed, and everything in it is in "natural" alignment.

Thus, too, the materials of nature, once invisible, are now truly seen. Formerly mute, they are now "heard." The rock, the stone, are placed in view; textures — bark, leaf, flower — are suddenly there. From this worked-over nature emerge the natural elements. Wood is carved with the grain so that the natural shape can assert itself. In the way the master sculptor Michelangelo said he worked, the Japanese carpenter finds the shape within the tree. Or, within the rock, for stone too has grain, and this the mason finds, chipping away to reveal the form beneath.

Made in Japan is a slogan we know, and one we now see has extensions — like silicon chips and carburetors. Not the same as carved wood or stone, but created by a similar impulse. And with such an unformulated national philosophy — nature is for use — it is not surprising. Everything is raw material, inanimate and animate as well.

Not only is nature so shaped, but human nature, too, is molded. We of the West may approve of the hand-dwarfed trees, the arranged flowers and the massaged beef, but we disapprove when people are given the same attention. Our tradition is against such control. Japan's, however, is not. It welcomes it. Society is supposed to form. Such is its function. We are (they would say) all of one family, all more or less alike. So we have our duties, our obligations. If we are to live contentedly, if society (our own construct) is to serve, then we must subject ourselves to its guiding pressures.

As the single finger bends the branch, so the social hand inclines the individual. If the unkempt tree is not considered natural, then the unkempt life is equally out of bounds. So, the Japanese do not struggle against the inevitable. And, as they say, alas, things cannot be helped, even when they can be. This simplified life allows them to follow their pursuits. These may be flower arranging, or

Zen, or *kendo* fencing. Or, on the other hand, working at Sony, Toyota, Honda. Or *is* it the other hand?

The support, the supported. The structure of Japanese society is visible, little is hidden. The unit is among those things most apparent. The module — tatami mats are all of a size, as are *fusuma* sliding doors and *shoji* paper panes. Mine fits your house, yours fits mine.

Socially, the module unit is the group. It is called the *nakama*. Each individual has many: family, school, club, company. Those inside *(naka)* form the group. This basic unit, the nakama, in its myriad forms, makes all of society. The wilderness, nature unformed and hence invisible, is outside the nakama of Japan, and that wilderness includes all nonmembers, among them, of course, us, the *gaijin* (foreigners). The West also has its family, its school, its company, but how flaccid, how lax. They lack the Japanese cohesion, the structural denseness, and at the same time the utter simplicity of design.

Land of the robot? Home of the bee and the ant? Given this functional and pragmatic structure, given this lack of dialectic (no active dichotomies — no good, no bad, no Platonic ideals at all), one might think so. But, no — it is something else. Let the Westerner sincerely try to live by Japanese custom, says Kurt Singer, Japan's most perspicacious observer, "and he will instantly feel what a cell endowed with rudiments of human sensibility must be supposed to feel in a well-coordinated body."

Does this not sound familiar? It is something we once all knew, we in the West as well. It is something like a balance between the individual and his society. One lives within social limitations to be sure. And if you do not have limitations, how do you define freedom? In Japan, the result is individual conformity: Each city, each house and each person is different from all the others yet essentially the same. The hand may shape the flower, but it is still a flower.

If one answer to the ambitions of immortality is to tear down and reconstruct exactly the Ise shrines, then one answer to the external problem of the one and the many (a Western dichotomy), to reconciling the demands of the individual and those of society, is the Japanese self in which the two selves become one. They are not, Japan proves, incompatible. The individual and that individual playing his social role are the same. As the house and the garden are the same. The nakama dissolves fast enough when wished — and freezes just as fast when desired. To see Japan then is to see an alternate way of thinking, to entertain thoughts we deem contradictionary. Having defined nature to his satisfaction, the Japanese may now lead what is for him a natural life.

This natural life consists of forming nature, of making reality. Intensely anthropomorphic, the Japanese is, consequently, intensely human. This also means curious, acquisitive, superstitious, conscious of self. There is an old garden concept (still to be seen at Kyoto's Ensu-ji temple) that is called *shakkei*. We translate it as ''borrowed scenery.'' The garden stops at a hedge. Beyond that hedge, space. Then in the distance — the mountain, Mount Hiei. It does not belong to the temple, but it is a part of its garden. The hand of the Japanese reaches out and enhances (appropriates) that which is most distant. Anything out there can become nature. The world is one, a seamless whole, for those who can see it; for those who can learn to observe, to regard, to understand.

—1984

Japanese Shapes

MAN IS THE ONLY one among the animals to make patterns, and among men, the Japanese are probably the foremost pattern-makers. They are a patterned people who live in a patterned country, a land where habit is exalted to rite; where the exemplar still exists; where there is a model for everything and the ideal is actively sought, where the shape of an idea or an action may be as important as its content; where the configuration of parts depends upon recognized form, and the profile of the country depends upon the shape of living.

The profile is visible — to think of Japan is to think of form. But beneath this, a social pattern also exists. There is a way to pay calls, a way to go shopping, a way to drink tea, a way to arrange flowers, a way to owe money. A formal absolute exists and is aspired to: social form must be satisfied if social chaos is to be avoided. Though other countries also have certain rituals that give the disordered flux of life a kind of order, here these become an art of behavior. It is reflected in the language, a tongue where the cliché is expected; there are formal phrases not only for meeting and for parting but also for begging pardon, for expressing sorrow, for showing anger, surprise, love itself.

This attachment to pattern is expressed in other ways: Japan is one of the last countries to wear costumes. Not only the fireman and the policeman, but also the student and the laborer. There is a suit for hiking, a costume for striking; there is the unmistakable fashion for the gangster and the indubitable ensemble of the fallen woman. In old Japan, the pattern was even more apparent: a fishmonger wore this, a vegetable seller, that; a samurai had his uniform as surely as a geisha had hers. The country should have resembled one of those picture scrolls of famous gatherings in which everyone is plainly labled; or one of those formal games — the chess-like *shogi* — in which is each piece is marked, moving in a predetermined way, recognized, each capable of just so much power.

More than the Arabs, more than the Chinese, the Japanese have felt the need for pattern and, hence, impose it. Confucious with his code of behavior lives on in Japan, not in China; the Japanese would probably have embraced the rigorous Koran had they known about it.

The triumph of form remains, however, mainly visual. Ritual is disturbed by the human; spontaneity ruins ethics. Japan thus makes patterns for the eyes and names are remembered only if read. Hearing is fallible; the eye is sure. Japan is the country of calling cards and forests of advertising: it is the land of the amateur artist and the camera. Everyone can draw, everyone can take pictures. The visual is not taught, it is known — it is like having perfect pitch.

To make a pattern is to discover one and copy it; a created form presumes an archetype. In Japan one suffers none of the claustrophobia of the Arab countries (geometrical wildernesses) and none of the dizzying multiplicity of America (every man his own creation) because the original model for the patterns of Japan was nature itself.

One still sees this from the air, a good introduction to the patterns of a country. Cultivated Japan is all paddies winding in free-form serpentine between the mountains, a quilt of checks and triangles on the lowlands — very different from the neat squares of Germany, or that vast and regular checkerboard of the United States. The Japanese pattern is drawn from nature. The paddy fields assume their shape because mountains are observed and valleys followed, because this is the country where the house was once made to fit into the curve of the landscape and where the farmer used to cut a hole in the roof rather than cut down the tree.

The natural was once seen as the beautiful and even now lip service is still given this thought. However, both then and now, the merely natural was never beautiful enough. That nature is grand only when it is natural — Byron's thought — would never have occurred to a Japanese. No, this ideal is closer to the ordered landscape of Byron's grandfather: forests become parks, trees are dwarfed, flowers are arranged. One does not go against nature but one takes advantage of it: one smooths, one embellishes. Nature is only the potential — man gives it is shape and meaning.

Since it is the natural forms that are traditionally most admired — the single rock, the spray of bamboo — it is these which are seen more frequently in Japanese art, delivered from the chaotic context of nature and given meaning through their isolation. There are canons but they derive from nature. Purple and red do not clash because, since they occur often enough in nature, no law of color can suggest that their proximity is unsatisfying. A single branch set at one side of the nichelike *tokonoma* and balanced by nothing is not ill-composed because there is a rule that insists that formal balance is not necessarily good. The Japanese garden is not the French: symmetry is something imposed upon nature, not drawn from it; asymmetry is a compromise between regularity and chaos.

To think of Japan is to think of form, because these patterns are repeated often and faithfully. Wherever the eye rests they occur. They give the look of the land a consistency, as though a set of rules had been rigorously followed.

It is these patterns, these shapes, these forms, these designs endlessly occurring, which mark the country. Chaos is vanquished; pattern prevails. They make the view more consistent than would otherwise have been possible — they create what often identifies art: style.

A pattern exists for everything: for temples, kimono, carpenters' saws, and the new is often in the shape of the old. There is only one way to build a shrine, to sew an *obi*. This traditional rigidity is in the outlines, the profile, and is based upon a geometry of stress and repose. In the decoration is individual variation: endless, myriad, protean invention. The shape of a temple bell remains but the patterned surface varies. Dressed stone, planed wood, decorated cloth or pottery, now the gleaming facets of plastic, chrome, glass — the surface is made visible by its own texture. The profile, austere and timeless, is metamorphosed into the unique, the individual.

Japanese design surprises, both in its extent and in its rightness. It is found in the castle and in the kitchen, and the combination of a nearly unvarying outline and a completely varying surface — a decoration which is all form — creates the kind of design that is weakly called "good."

Not however until recently by the Japanese themselves. Traditional design was never noticed. We, the curious foreigners, are in a better position. On the other hand, if we had never seen and did not know the use of some of our own more lovely objects — the light bulb, the toilet bowl, the spoon — we would possibly find them beautiful. But habit blinds and practical knowledge usually deprives of vision. Japan is still distant enough from us that essence is perceived. Disassociated from function, the object become formal rather than practical; it becomes a complete entity, and its visual character is all there is.

Design is a matter of economics, and an unchanging economy creates an unchanging design. Usually this design is the conjunction of the nature of the material plus the least possible effort. Japanese design is inseparable from art in that it is rarely the least effort but the most. Consequently, Japanese craftsman are paid almost as much as artists would be, as anyone now wishing to construct a real Japanese-style house soon discovers. In Tokugawa Japan, as in eighteenth-century England, one is continually surprised that the gentry spent its money so well.

This economy not only produced the audience for craft, it also maintained it, and the standards of the craftsmanship itself. So long as the economy remained undisturbed there could be no question of fashion. For two and a half centuries the country was closed and even before that there was — except, of course, for the massive cultural importations from China and Korea — little foreign (Western) influence, that great fashion-maker. From the age of Shakespeare to the time of Tennyson, through all the French Louis' and all the British Georges,' Japan isolated itself. Until Meiji, the latter half of the nineteenth century, Japan had no arches, corner-stones, fireplaces, armchairs or farthingales.

Thus, Japan had never had to contend with the old-fashioned. It had never seen an entire style wane and then wax again. Since old things continued to be used, except for the minor surface variations there was no concept of the structurally old. There were no antique stores, only second-hand stores. Precious, old objects existed but always in the context of the present.

These old things showed the same "perfect" shape. They accommodated themselves both to their desired use and also to the natural laws of stress and respose. Design followed the Confucian standard in all things: uniformity and authority. It followed that Japan is thus the home of the module unit, the first of the pre-fab lands. At the same time, though the profile is standard, individuality is allowed, insisted upon, on the surface itself. One might say of Japanese art as Aldous Huxley said of the Mayan: ". . . it is florid but invariably austere, a more chaste luxuriance was never imagined."

Although the distinction between outline profile and surface decoration is as artificial and as arbitrary as that between form and content, it is possible to say that Japanese design not only permits but insists upon archetypal patterns and all such patterns show a like division, a like propensity.

This natural affinity everywhere remains. Lewis Mumford has observed that the airplane is called beautiful because it looks like a seagull. In Japan this affinity is more acknowledged, more displayed, than elsewhere. Thus, one of the reasons for the beauty of Japanese design, its rightness, its fitness, and one of the reason for the proliferation of Japanese forms, their economy, their enormous presence, is that the Japanese man and woman, artist or not, is among the last to forget the earliest lesson which nature teaches all makers.

—1962

Japanese Rhythms

CULTURES HAVE their own rhythms: how they divide the days and the nights, when to go fast and when to go slow, in what manner to fragment time.

Some of the differences are familiar. A well-known temporal gulf exists between the global north and south. The latter have, for example, their famous siesta — night again in the middle of the day. The northern visitor is always surprised at this diurnal difference, and often irritated as well. What? The post office isn't open? Don't these people know it is two in the afternoon?

Another familiar gulf, this time a chasm, exists also between East and West, the Orient and the Occident. We speak of the slower pace, calling it leisurely if we like it, indolent if we do not. Our travel brochures advise us to go and, specifically, *relax* in exotic such-and-such.

These various temporal differences are well known. Not so familiar are those cultures which blend the differences and bridge the gulfs. Among these, the most spectacular is Japan. Here the rhythms of the West have been rigorously applied and yet, under these, the old pulse of Asia is still strongly felt.

Seen from the outside, the way that the Japanese structure time seems much closer to New York than, say, Kandy or Mandalay. Indeed, most of the Western temporal virtues — efficiency, promptness, get-up-and-go — are being flung in our faces by this seemingly industrious nation.

Yet, the view from the inside indicates that older, more purely Asian rhythms persist. There is the new way of arranging the day and then there is the old. And these two, as with so much else in Japan, coexist — strata in time.

Early to bed, early to rise, etc., has been the recipe for business success in the WASP world and this is the image (bright-eyed and bushy-tailed) that such have had of themselves. Thus, the Japanese, taking over this image and making it theirs, now insist that they are a hard-working people and are more flattered than wounded when called workaholics. Such a role means rising at dawn, rushing to the office, putting in long hours, racing home and going to bed early to rest for the next fulfilling day.

Since this is the official version, it is officially supported. And since everyone has nominally gone home, buses stop running at ten-thirty; the subways stop at midnight, and the trains shut down half an hour later. Unlike that of New York and Paris, shameless night-owl abodes, Japanese civic transportation does not run all night long.

Yet, the populace is no more off the streets at twelve now than it was in old Tokugawa Japan. The entertainment districts are filled with people long after midnight. These are not at home resting for the next busy day. They are getting around the night spots by taking taxis.

Nor do the Japanese actually get up at dawn. Indeed, nowadays, a majority does not get to work until ten o'clock, also the hour when the bazaar at Rangoon opens. To be sure, some attempt an earlier arrival. Being first into the office in the morning supports, and in part creates, the modern idea of the Japanese as being very hard workers.

And the last out as well. One is supposed to hang around even though one's work may be finished. Being one of the group is considered important and rushing out to conform to an egotistical timetable is bad modern form. Rather, one subscribes to the group timetable. This has nothing to do with working hard. It has to do merely with attendance.

Indeed, as one looks more closely at the manner in which modern Japan structures the business day, one becomes very aware of the differences between modern and traditional timekeeping and how these intermingle.

Once the modern rush to the office is over and the business day is actually begun, the time scheme becomes traditional. There is lots of discussion, lots of stopping to drink tea — and nowadays lots of visits to the ubiquitous coffee shop to talk some more. Nor is this talk confined to work in the narrow Western sense of the term. Rather, work is socialized, and social talk can serve as work because its larger purpose is the cementing of personal relations.

The amount of time spent at what we in the West would call work is much less than what one might expect. The notorious efficiency of Japan does not depend upon time spent. Rather, it depends upon absence of intermural conflict, lots of intramural competition, and an ideological solidarity which is almost beyond the comprehension of Europe and America. This is of use mainly (or merely) in the hours, days, years spent together — in the creation and continuation of the group. This is equally true when the office is left. It is often left as a group since no one wishes to break cohesion by leaving first. Then the group divides into sub-groups which then go out on the town, to favorite pubs and bars, to continue the social amelioration which has traditionally been so important to Japan.

Far from early-to-bed, the upwardly mobile Japanese male is

fortunate if he catches the last train home. And often he will stay overnight with an office friend, an event that his wife back home will accept as a part of the normal rhythm of her spouse.

She may even encourage the event. I know of one young office worker who would like nothing better than to leave his company conferers and return to wife and child. But this she discourages because if he were seen by the neighbors coming home early they would certainly gossip, and the rumor would spread that he was not properly getting on in his company career.

In places where day and night are divided strictly according to the needs of actual work — I don't know, let's say, Chicago — the pattern may be closer to the ideal of which Japan brags. As it is, Japanese temporal reality is something different — far closer to that of Bangkok or Jakarta, the rest of Asia, places where time is almost by definition something which is spent together.

That a good deal of time in Japan is wasted (endless tea and coffee breaks, lots of after-hours in cabarets) is a Western, not a Japanese criticism. Japan never considers time together as time wasted. Rather, it is time invested.

Yet, for a culture as time-conscious as Japan (one sees mottos on office walls: Time is Money), the amount of real temporal waste is surprising. Here, too, the country shows its ancient Asian roots.

Take the matter of appointments for example. In the big business world of the West being punctual is sacrosanct. Again, actuality may be another matter, but all subscribe to the idea that to be on time is to be good.

In Asia, however, this is not so. One is frequently left cooling one's heels in the great capitals of the Orient. And here Japan, despite its Western temporal veneer, is no different. If you are meeting a member of your group, then he will wait and you can be late. If you are meeting a non-member you can also be late because it is not so important whether you meet or not.

Spatially, the Japanese are very efficient regarding rendezvous. There are known places to meet. In Tokyo one meets in front of Shinjuku's Kinokuniya Bookstore, in front of Ginza's Wako Department Store, in front of the Almond Coffee Shop at Roppongi, and at Shibuya in front of the statue of Hachiko, famous loyal dog who waited there for years for its dead master.

Most waiting Japanese are in the position of Hachiko. It is rare to observe anyone being on time. Indeed, it appears as though one portion of the nation (smaller) is punctilious and that the rest (larger) is flagrantly errant.

Those who are on time and are doing the waiting are those in an inferior position (in Japan it is the girls who wait on the boys and not the other way about) or those who want something from the late arrival. Time is money, indeed — but then, come to think of it, the motto is written usually in English and in a Japanese situation only Japanese is operative. For all this show of making appointments, Japanese standards of punctuality are closer to those of Samarkand than of Paris or London.

Still, one wonders. With time so precious that it must be doled out in little pieces, must be compared to legal tender, how then can it be so wantonly wasted?

Well, it is not one's own time that is being wasted, to be sure. It is the other person's, he or she who is waiting. In fact, one's own time supply is somewhat short. That is why one is late, you see.

We in the West who make nothing like the fuss about time that the Japanese do, would be mortally insulted to be kept waiting, let us say, an hour. Yet many Japanese would wait an hour, standing by store, coffee shop or bronze dog.

And is this not perhaps then the largest difference between the time concept of East and West? Time is not moral in Asia; it cannot be used as a weapon. (Do you realize that you have kept me waiting for fifteen minutes?) And it cannot really be used to indicate virtue (hard-working, efficient) or vice (lax, late for appointments).

It is rather a seamless entity, an element like the air in which we live. To live naturally with time, says Asia, is to pay no attention to it. And Japan, despite its modernization, still subscribes to this ancient tradition. Dig down through company minutes and office hours and there, firm, eternal, is time itself.

—1984

II

Tokyo, the Impermanent Capital

THOUGH THE CITIES of Japan, particularly Tokyo, appear to the foreign visitor to be reassuringly (or distressingly) Western, acquaintance with these modern-seeming urban complexes indicates that they are not Western nor, indeed, in any Western sense, modern. There are the high-rise structures, the elevated highway networks, and the proliferating suburbs all familiar to the West, but the city functions in a completely un-Western manner. Tokyo may look like Los Angeles but, as the visitor soon discovers, it does not act like it.

The first indication of this occurs when the Western visitor attempts to find his way about the city. He assumes that any city is planned and that there is a logic, however obscured, to be discerned in its structure. Tokyo, however, exhibits nothing of the sort. Most of the streets, for example, are not named, though all the crossings are; the plots are not numbered, though the houses are, with the result that addresses (assigned to houses in order of their construction date rather than their locations) are much scrambled; though districts are numbered, the numbering plan is arbitrary.

There is also little of the civic convenience observed in Western cities — few large central parks, no real congregation of cultural facilities. Likewise there is no zoning — no slums and no ghettos, no good and bad sides of the tracks, no strictly industrial areas, no strictly wealthy residential districts. Instead, rich and poor live side by side, and the bank, the pinball parlor, the beauty shop and the ward office are found in juxtapositions which are sometimes incongruous to Western ideas.

All of this is because the overall plan, the civic ordering of the city is missing. There is no imposed and consequently logical pattern such as one sees in the West — and also in Kyoto, Japan's only ordered city. There is much of the natural patterning one discovers in any living, growing organism, but this does not assist the confused Westerner who eventually must discover that the only way to travel profitably about the city is to memorize it.

Once this is accomplished, however, and once the visitor begins to accustom himself to Tokyo, he discovers that both patterns and structures are, in fact, evident — ones, however, he would not find in a modern Western city. There, units are welded together to create residential areas, business areas, etc. Here, these units are independent.

This difference is apparent in the cityscape of Tokyo itself. From any tall building one may look out over the vastness of the metropolis and find that there seems many more units — single buildings — than in Western cities. A view of Tokyo is like a pointilistic painting, each dot apparently unattached to the other, each building seemingly alone and independent. Individual architectural styles, building to building, greatly differ and no attempt is made toward any kind of visual cohesion.

As the visitor looks and learns, however, he sees that these variegated units are actually grouped, though not in the way he would expect in a city. The single units form small complexes. In each there is a bank, a supermarket, a flower shop, a pinball parlor. What one sees when one looks closely at Tokyo is a collection of hundreds of villages.

Each is a small town and their numbers make up this enormous capital. Like cells in a body, each contains identical elements, and the resulting pattern is an organic one. No town planner has touched this natural order.

Here the visitor may remember a similar city-structure with which he is familiar: the feudal European town. It too simply grew and assumed a final form natural to its inhabitants. Or he may remember Arab communities which still take this form — growing out from the market place or the railway station. In the same sense the Japanese city, composed of many of these units, remains natural — or primitive.

Just as the Japanese themselves can — and perhaps should — be seen as a tribe, or a collection of tribes (Gregory Clark's excellent idea), so their cities may be seen as integrated ensembles of small communities. This is as true of such smaller collections as Sapporo and Kagoshima as it is of the megapolis which now extends from Tokyo—Yokohama to Osaka—Kyoto. Each community has its usually identical parts — the general store or the department store branch, the specialized food shops (butcher, rice dealer, vegetable seller, fruit store) and its places of leisure (the coffee shop, the bar, the neighborhood theater, etc.). And these are much like those in the neighboring communities. Indeed as in the module-built traditional Japanese house (*tatami, shoji, fusuma,* always in the same size), all the parts seem interchangeable. And each unit is, within the confines of its genre, complete.

Complete and impermanent. The observing visitor, turning from spatial to temporal considerations, soon sees that though nowadays such materials as stone, steel, brick and marble are widely used, the city as a whole does not appear as though it were built to last. In the days of wood and tile the very nature of the materials implied a certain mortality. Now, though the building materials have changed, their fallibility still seems assumed.

This air of the transient in otherwise permanent-seeming buildings is enforced in that traditional Japanese architectural styles are now largely neglected. Rather, new buildings in Japanese cities are constructed in styles so flamboyantly modern that one cannot but expect them to be shortly superceded. The air of unreality is consequently strong.

Also, no alternate unity of architectural style is attempted or achieved. Just as the Japanese himself is often meticulous about his family or his group, but neglects what we might define as his civic duties, so his buildings are units complete within themselves, no attempt being made to harmonize these with either the setting or the adjacent structures. Hence the random appearance of the Japanese city — no zoning, no attempt to create an overall district style, nothing but one individual expression after another. The unreality for the Westerner lies partly in that his assumptions about urban grammar are not those of the Japanese.

Consequently Japanese cities feel to him like the back lots of movie studios where the various sets, all of them quite large and seemingly permanent, are constructed, used, and left standing. There seems no reason for their arrangement. They were built where they are for reasons of economy and convenience. There is no unifying style because the uses for each were different. And though they look sturdy one knows that they were not made to last and that, indeed, they will not.

The Western social structure which a city such as Tokyo most resembles is the single "city" which the West erects with full knowledge that it is not supposed to last. This is the exposition. Massive buildings are thrown up, streets are made, vast crowds are accommodated, but only for a season. The assumption is that all this will be pulled down. Consequently, building only for now, architects are traditionally encouraged to be both contemporary and extreme. Thus Tokyo is like an international exposition which has remained standing. If city structure in Japan remains "primitive," then these extremely contemporary-looking structures are like the tents of the nomads — with the difference that the Japanese move not in space but in time.

One ought further examine this concept of the "primitive" and at the same time deprive it of its pejorative aspect. There is small doubt that the Japanese cities represent a stage of urban development earlier than that represented by those of the contemporary West. The concept is both simpler and, in its way, more natural. Certainly, once studied, the Japanese city is easier to comprehend than the Western. One can see the various village-units that make up the town-units; one can understand how these amalgamate into the city. In America, unless one understood the complicated social and economic forces involved, one could not comprehend why the main shopping districts should be moved from the center of town to its outlying suburbs, why this ring city should have no central section, and why there is little or no public transportation to such distant areas. The Western city is certainly the more highly evolved and the more difficult to understand. It is in this sense the more "civilized." Its assumptions are, also, entirely different.

A Western assumption is that the city is logically planned and built to last. Each structure in it is presumed to be in its proper place and constructed to endure. It is believed that what a man builds his descendants will enjoy. The urban complex may be added to, individual buildings may be replaced, the structure itself may be altered, but the assumption remains that, once built, it remains intrinsically as it was. This is accepted as literally true and the architect correspondingly builds for the future.

An Eastern assumption, seen particularly in the cities of Japan and especially in its capital, Tokyo, is quite different. The city is not planned and all the buildings in it are subject to almost routine renewal. Opportunities to redesign the city — earthquakes, fires, wartime bombings — are ignored and solid buildings younger than those who live in them are pulled down to make way for new. The assumption is that the city itself is transient, and the architect consequently builds for the present.

The Western city also assumes immortality. Buildings are made to last. (This is also true of many non-Western cities as well, Beijing for example.) Behind the assumption of this somewhat illogical immortality (since man and his works are nothing if not mortal) lies another concept. This is that one ''ought'' to appear immortal in all of one's edifices. Anything which is made must be made for the ages. This in turn implies an amount of striving. The state strived for (and many Western architectural styles indicate this — think of soaring Gothic architecture) is something-more-than-human. Dissatisfied with the common state, the Westerner attempts to deny it. (As do official cities in the East — Beijing is solid as the pyramids; in the Chinese countryside, however, peasants continue to build in mortal clay.) This denial is responsible for some architectural wonders. It is also responsible for Los Angeles.

Asians — and particularly the Japanese — have not (or have not until recently) shared such assumptions. Indeed, the assumptions have been just the opposite. Impermanence is our natural state and transience is the prime quality of life. There is merely constant sameness within constant change, and it is this quality which creates what small permanence the Japanese can observe.

The great shrine at Ise is torn down once every twenty years. The wooden building demolished, its replica — identical in all respects — is constructed adjacent. Two decades later, when the new building is now old and weathered, it too is destroyed and a structure precisely similar is erected on the land the older building formerly occupied. This has been going on for centuries and indicates Japan's accommodating answer to the demands of immortality.

In its way the Japanese city follows this same pattern. The idea of continually pulling down and putting up is very strong. Tokyo for this reason always seems under construction and, indeed, will never be finally finished. The "logic" of the Japanese city lies just in this temporal consideration. Its assumption (so unlike that of the Western city which can be seen to live entirely in its past) is that the "now" is important but the importance of this "now" lies well within the framework of the accepted permanence within continual change. Tokyo buildings are consequently always new and yet, in this sense, always the same.

Which kind of city best suits human beings is a question which must be individually answered. Certainly Tokyo, with its villages and towns inside the central city, its convenience, fits a society where the family and the other social units remain important. At the same time its systems of public transportation make traveling from one section of this enormous city to another both possible and convenient. It is one of the few major cities where one does not want to own a car. Tokyo would seem to lack, however, any of those architectural monuments which speak so eloquently of timelessness, of immortality — except, as we have seen, in the concept of timeless impermanence which the Japanese city has incorporated into itself.

The Western visitor is thus present with an anomaly when he visits a city such as Tokyo. He finds a completely humanized city, in that the more-than-human is never stressed and the merely-human is always emphasized. At the same time he cannot understand the natural and organic form of the city precisely because structural logic has no place in such a form. Nor is Tokyo, despite all of its bustle and seeming contemporaneity, a city which makes modern (logical) assumptions. That one can never locate an address in the city without outside (policeman, postman, tobacco-stand woman) help would indicate that it is not in any Western sense an efficient urban complex. But then efficiency as a virtue is not a Japanese concept.

What the visitor discovers, if he stays long enough, is a city which, despite its strangeness, is somehow familiar to him. He may then remember that its pattern is that of his own hometown — if he came from a hometown small enough.

—1979

The 'Real' Disneyland

LOOKING AT TOKYO one sometimes wonders why the Japanese went to all the trouble of franchising a Disneyland in the suburbs when the capital itself is so superior a version.

Disneyland, and the other lands it has spawned, is based upon the happy thought of geographical convenience: all the interesting localities on earth located at one spot. Thus, there are African rivers and Swiss mountains and Caribbean islands and American towns. One feels one is seeing the world in miniature and, indeed, "it's a small world" is the slogan of one of the concessions.

Compare this now to Tokyo. There are hundreds of American fast-food stands with matching mock-Colonial architecture, there is a plaster Fontana di Trevi and a state guest house modeled after Versailles; there are dozens of red lacquered Chinese restaurants and equal numbers of white stuccoed Italian; there are thousands of boutiques with famous foreign names (Gucci, Dior, Yves St. Laurent, Arnold Palmer) printed all over them; there is an imitation Baker Street straight from London; the Museum of Western Art in Ueno has Rodin castings all over the front yard; and there is even an onion-domed Russian Orthodox cathedral. All of this, and much more, in a glorious architectural confusion of Corinthian columns and chromium pylons, dormer windows and curved escalators, half-timber, plain red brick, sheet steel, textured lucite.

In this architectural stew (something from every place on earth) even the authentically Japanese takes on the pleasant flavor of ersatz novelty. Thus the old Toshogu Shrine in Ueno or the Awashimado (1618) in Asakusa appear in Tokyo's Disneyland context just as pleasingly synthetic as the new Japanese modern-style restaurant gotten up almost right as a French bistro.

In the face of this massive transplantation of everywhere else right into the heart of the capital, the Disney enterprises would seem to face the stiffest of competition. Tokyo is a mammoth Disneyland with an area of nearly 2,500 sq. km., and a working staff of almost 12 million. Yet not only Tokyo but all of Japan seems always to have the time (and the money) for the little imported Disneyland perched on reclaimed land in the outskirts.

One of the reasons would be that Japan is the real home of all such concepts as Disneyland has come to exemplify. To go there is, in a way, to come home. It was in Japan, after all, that the concept of the microcosm has been most fully elaborated, from its beginnings right down to Walkman-type baby loudspeakers for the ears, the wrist-watch TV, and the smallest and fastest silicon chip yet.

Japan, too, has also displayed a fondness for the geographical microcosm, the bringing together of famous places into a single locality. Look at the number of little towns in Japan that sport a Ginza, plainly a replica of what was once Tokyo's most famous shopping street. And look at the number of gardens that have a little Mount Fuji, small but climbable, included among their attractions.

Indeed the classical Japanese garden gives ready indication of how dear the microcosmic impulse has long been to the Japanese heart, and how early the Japanese had perfected these small visitable worlds.

Take, for example, the Korakuen in Tokyo — an Edo-period garden. One climbs a small hill which calls itself Mount Lusha in

China, and finds oneself at a replica of the Togetsu bridge from
Kyoto's Arashiyama district. But the view is not the river but
Hangzhou's famous lake — we are back in China again. Not for
long, however; climb another hill and here is Kyoto once more,
the veranda platform of the Kiyomizu Temple, one of the famous
sights of the city.

Some Edo gardens are even more Disneyland-like. For example
Tokyo's Rikugien in Komagome. Here, in one place, arranged
somewhat like a miniature golf course, are all of the 88 classical
sites, all tiny, and all with noticeboards explaining the Chinese or
Japanese association.

Lest it be thought that all of this is just big-city Tokyo and late
Edo commercialism, Japan's claim to early Disneyfication must be
defended. Did you know that the garden of the elegant Katsura
Villa is itself a miniaturization of famous scenic attractions from
elsewhere — that there is the Sumiyoshi pine, and the Tsutsumi
waterfall, and the Oigawa river, and the famous wooded spit on
the other side of Japan, Ama no Hashidate? And that even the
elegant moss-garden, that of Saihoji, contains — if one knows
how to find them — scenes from ten famous places, reproductions
of ten famous things (rocks, etc.), ten poetic references, and ten
famous pine trees — all reproductions, fancied though they be, of
something somewhere else?

Even Ryoan-ji's famous rock garden has its Disney attributes.
Those rocks — what are they, besides being just rocks? Well,
they are various things. They are manifestations of the infinite, or
they are islands in the ocean, a section of the famous Inland Sea.
Or (a very Disney touch, this) they are a mother tiger and her
frolicking cubs.

Even earlier, the avatar of Walt Disney was alive and well in Japan. He would have loved the Byodo-in, replica of a Chinese water pavilion, with imitation Chinese swan-boats (phoenixes, actually) being poled and pushed about. And he would have noted with pleasure that in gardens of the period everything was always something else — something from far away. One way of arranging garden rocks in inland Kyoto was *suhama* (graveled seashore) and another was *ariso* (rocky beaches).

Earlier yet, Japanese gardens were displaying the vision that later made Disneyland famous. Here in the first gardens what do we find? Why, things from far away indeed. The garden was a representation of Sukhavati, the Western Paradise of the Buddha Amitabha. And those rocks in the water were the three islands of the blessed — Horai, Hojo and Eishu. And that big rock in the middle — that is Mount Sumera itself.

The date of this kind of garden is 1000. Just think — almost 1000 years ago Japanese vision and technique had in Sumera made the first Space Mountain!

It is evident that the Japanese claim to prior Disneyfication is a very strong one. No other country has brought the principle of the microcosm — ikebana, bonsai, *chanoyu,* gardens — to such profuse perfection. No other has managed to turn so much into something else.

So, when one wonders why Japan, such a Disneyland itself, needed a real Disneyland, one must conclude that it found here something in which a true fellow-feeling was discovered. And also, perhaps, because in Disneyland it recognized as well one of its own enduring qualities.

This is a passion amounting to near genius for kitsch. If kitsch

is defined as primarily something pretending to be something else
— wood acting like marble, plastic acting like flowers, Anaheim,
California acting like the Mississippi — then Japan has a long
history, a celebrated expertise and a strong claim to mastery in
just this very thing. In fact, Japan often enough has been called
"the home of kitsch."

If this is true then, with understandable enthusiasm Japan embraced the biggest piece of kitsch in the West. Did so, then broke
off a chunk and brought it home to add to its collection.

—1985

The City Home

THE JAPANESE appear to regard their homes in a manner somewhat different from us in the West. In the United States there is the tradition that a man's home is his castle, much is made of the homemade meal, and it is agreed no other place is like home. In Japan, a man's castle is usually his office, the simply homemade is often garnished with the more elegantly store-bought, and there are many places which are like home and are treated as such.

With so little attention being paid to home, it is not surprising that Japanese dwellings suffer by comparison. Foreign diplomats even call them rabbit hutches. This description is perhaps occasioned by the fact that Japanese homes are small and crowded and not, as it would first appear, that they are units used mainly for sleeping.

The living space is much less than that enjoyed by others of equal income in other countries. Whole families are crammed into one or two LDKs — the abbreviation for living room, dining room and kitchen squeezed into single or multiple units. The units themselves come in various sizes, none of them large. A san-jo is a three tatami-mat room, a hachi-jo is eight. Tatami mats used to be six by three feet in area, but the newer apartment-sized mats are much smaller. Thus a family of four living in a roku-jo (six-mat) LDK does enjoy a somewhat rabbit-like intimacy.

In the old days before Japan became affluent, four people could perhaps have coped with such restricted space. Bedding and clothing were put out of sight in closets and the tokonoma alcove would hold a space-suggesting flower arrangement. Now,

however, the Japanese have become the world's foremost con-
sumers and buying begins at home. Thus into this room is stuffed
the washing machine, the fridge and the freezer, the color TV set,
the children's bunk beds, the piano and anything else which the
family has been induced to buy. A consequence is that space is
much restricted and a somewhat hutch-like appearance results.

Another consequence is that space has become the greatest luxury to which a Japanese can aspire. It used to be time. Anyone
well enough off not to work on Sundays was considered a kind of
temporal millionaire. Everyone else, the temporal poor, worked
every day with just one day off a month. Now in the new age of
affluence, none (except store employees and they get a compen-
satory weekday off) work on Sundays and progressively fewer
work on Saturdays as well. Affluence and leisure are now enjoyed
by a majority, except that now if you stay at home there is no
space in which to enjoy either.

I am, to be sure, describing city conditions. In the country, one
might afford a larger apartment or perhaps a house or maybe even
the greatest of contemporary luxuries, a garden. But now well
over half of all Japanese live in cities and the *kukan mondai* or space
problem affects a majority. Space in any quantity is not to be had
except at the most extravagant of prices.

The cost of housing is mainly due, of course, to the postwar
rush to the cities, but this has occurred in other countries as well,
with results not so spectacularly cramped as those of Tokyo or
Osaka. There would perhaps have been ways of using the
available land so that more attractive if not more spacious living
units could have been created. But the square apartment block
with its thousands of square little rooms was the design decided

upon and some of the results in suburban *danchi* (housing developments) are more chicken coop than rabbit hutch.

Perhaps one of the reasons for this is the attitude which the Japanese have toward their dwellings. Far from being a castle, a Japanese man's home often seems merely a place where the wife and kids are kept. It is a kind of base for the husband to operate from, a place where he stores his clothes and where he sleeps. Though consumer interests have tried to make something profitable out of the less proprietary *My Car, My House* (in that telling order, incidentally) even the use of the gregarious "my," instead of the egotistical *watakushi no* (my own), has failed to reverberate except for a time among the very young and the newly married. Tradition, certain kinds of tradition, remains strong, and home is still merely father's home base.

As a consequence, the Japanese male rarely complains about rabbit-hutchery. He is there only a third of a 24-hour day and unconscious during most of that time, and he also has many alternate homes. The one who really suffers is the wife. She is stuck in her crowded roku-jo day in and day out and can rarely leave her claustrophobic danchi dwelling except to join the throngs at the supermarket. If she seldom complains, it is only because Japanese women seldom complain about anything.

The Japanese male attitude toward the home (and there are many telling exceptions to these generalizations I am strewing about) is that it is but one of the many stations in his busy day (and night). He spends much more walking time at the office than he does at home (which does not say, of course, that he does not also catnap at the office) and, since so much Japanese business consists of businessmen entertaining each other, he spends an unusually large amount of time in bars, night clubs, cabarets and the like.

The phenomenon of going out with the boys for an evening is also known in the West. There, it is greeted with some suspicion, if not cynicism. In Japan, however, it is known that there is no better way of cementing those all important inter/intra-office relations than not going home of an evening but of enjoying a bit of night life together.

Back home the wife will already have made the supper (since the husband, traditionally at any rate, is far too busy to let her know whether he is coming home to eat it or not), and she and the kids will be consuming it.

It is here that one might remark upon a remarkable aspect of the attitude toward home: the Japanese male enjoys a plurality of homes. It is not only the roku-jo, it is also the office, the favorite bar, the favorite coffee shop. He tends to be "at home" in any of the many places he chooses to be.

This attitude, in turn, has created the thousands of bars within the cities and, one would think, the tens of thousands of coffee shops. These are places where business is discussed but they are also, for the time being, home itself. It is perhaps for this reason that the vast majority of bars are so-called *bottle-keep* establishments. That is, the known customer (and there are no unknown customers in the better Japanese bars) has a part of himself — his own private bottle, decorated with his name — in this alternate home. In the coffee shop he has his own favorite table, and the help had better realize this as soon as possible. He is, in other words, making his own a number of locations which the West does not regard as particularly homelike.

It is telling, I think, that the Japanese language does not have a word for "home," or, at least, a word with such Anglo-American associations. *Ie* means "house," not home, and though *uchi* has homelike possibilities it does not invariably carry the warmer nuances of such redolent phrases as "home, sweet home." Indeed, a Japanese cannot, strictly speaking, be homesick. He can only be hometown-sick, and the nostalgic word is not uchi but *furu-sato,* the home town — again, a plurality.

The Japanese male's attitude toward home has thus conditioned and created a number of urban attributes in contemporary society. The extended family (the in-laws) was sacrificed with an almost unseemly hastle when the kukan mondai made the so-called nuclear family (papa, mama, two kids) the only economical unit. The necessary garden was similarly dismissed (along with the whole idea of Japan's symbiotic attitude toward nature) when both space and economic considerations made it an impossibility.

On the other hand tradition, when it is useful, is maintained and even strengthened. The Japanese city has always had more bars than the non-Japanese city. These have proliferated to an amazing degree. The foreign visitor, surprised at the number of bars in the cities, wonders that any of them make any money, so fierce would seem the competition. They do, however, because half the population are customers and because these customers, having found a home, are loyal to it. And this was as true in Edo as it is in Tokyo.

Though the ubiquitous coffee shop is largely a postwar phenomenon, it has been — as its sheer number indicates — incorporated into the home-away-from-home syndrome. It could even be called the daytime bar, serving as a home-substitute

the same as its nocturnal equivalent, were it not that here —
finally — the female, wife or not, finds her own piece of homelike
territory. Though wives do often entertain other wives in their
proper homes, the coffee shop offers an attractive alternative.

The coffee shop seems to know this. It is quite different from
the European coffee shop. Always snugly enclosed (no open-air
terraces in Japan), it contains curtains, easy chairs, personalized
coffee cups, an array of newspapers and magazines, air condition-
ing, lots of green plants — in short, it contains everything the
Japanese home is supposed to contain and, due to space limitations, often does not.

Here, as in eighteenth-century English coffee houses — more
clubs than shops — men gather to discuss. And here, unlike the
eighteenth-century English coffee houses, the women also gather.
Each is finding solace and space. Each is experiencing that unique-
ly Japanese phenomenon (unique in scope at least): the alternate
and substitute home.

It would thus seem true indeed that the Japanese regard the
concept of home in a different manner. Home is regarded, if one
cares to put it this way, in a creative manner. Since home itself is
not actually lived in but merely visited by the male, alternate
home-substitutes have been created along his daily path. The liabili-
ty of rabbit-hutch homes has been turned, in a very Japanese manner, into a kind of asset — a plurality of homes.

How destructive this is to wife, children and the concept of
family — since home is, according to Western ideas, more than a
place to sleep — is problematical. Byron has said that "without
hearts there is no home." He was thinking perhaps of the extended family; he was certainly not thinking of the Japanese nuclear

family. At the same time, however, he was talking about closeness, family warmth and, I suppose, familial love. It is not that this does not exist in the contemporary Japanese family; just that conditions for its generation are no longer ideal.

—1980

Walking in Tokyo

ONE WALKS FOR various reasons. Often it is to get somewhere. Occasionally it is to enjoy the walk. The street leads someplace. Usually it is seen as a stretch connecting one place with another. Sometimes it is seen as itself. Different cities have different streets. The differences depend upon how the street is used and how it is seen. That is, walking in Marrakesh is different from walking in, say, Chicago.

And walking in Tokyo is different from either. Streets here have their mundane and ostensible uses but they also have something more. The Japanese street remains Asian, and it is still, in a number of senses, an area of display.

As, to be sure, are the streets of other cities. One thinks of the *plaka*, the town square, the café-lined avenue. But there are differences. In Europe, one is part of the display — to see and be seen, to look and be looked at. The street is a stage. How different Japan. There are no European-style cafés, few American-style malls. And usually no place to sit down. You, the walker, are not an actor.

Rather, you are an active spectator. The display is not you and the others about you. The display is the street itself. The direction is not from you to it but from it to you.

Shops line the street, open up, spill out. Clothes on racks and sides of beef alike are shoved onto sidewalks. The fish shop's scaly glitter is right there, still gasping. Baby televisions piled high blink at you, eye to eye. Not here the closed transactions of the supermarket. Rather, on the Tokyo street, there is the raw profusion of consumption itself.

And even in the more sedate avenues, such as the Ginza, where goods stay indoors, the display continues. Signs and flags proclaim; *kanji* (Chinese ideographs) grab and neon points. Signs, signs everywhere, all of them shouting, a semiotic babble, signifiers galore, all reaching out to the walker, the person going past.

This is what is very Asian about the Japanese street. This we would recognize if the units were mangoes or rice cakes. But here they are calculators and microwave ovens, instant cameras and word processors. The content startles.

Yet the form reassures. This is, even yet, the Japanese street we see in Hokusai and read about in Saikaku. In old Edo the main street was called the *noren-gai*. The better shops advertised themselves with their *noren*, those entry curtains marked with the shop crest. The noren-gai was the better stretch where worth and probity were the standards.

The concept remains. The noren may be facade-high neon or a mile-long laser beam, but the *gai* (district) is still marked as the place of display. From Ginza's store-window showcases to the piles of silicon chips out on the sidewalk — like exotic nuts — in Akihabara, the display continues, a year-round drama in which all the actors are for sale.

The Japanese street is, in a way, the ideal to which all other streets must aspire. It is the ultimate in unrestrained display. Other streets in other countries are handicapped by zoning laws and citizen's associations and the like. Not so Tokyo, or not to that extent. The Japanese street is very public.

Conversely, the Japanese home is very private. In Edo all the houses had high fences. In Tokyo, though suburbia must content itself with merely a token hedge, privacy remains much respected. The house and the garden (if there is one) are private property in the most closed and restricted sense. In a city as crowded as Tokyo — Edo, too, for that matter — privacy is a luxury almost as expensive as space. What is acquired at great expense is zealously guarded.

What is enclosed is, thus, private property. And what is open is not — it is public. So it is with most Western cities as well. But in Japan the difference is that the public space appears to belong to no one; it seems to be no one's responsibility. As a consequence, there are few effective zoning laws, very little civic endeavor, almost no city planning, and while housing is subject to scrutiny, the surrounding streets are not.

And so, the streets of Tokyo are allowed an organic life of their own. They grow, proliferate; on all sides street life takes on unrestricted natural forms.

Tokyo is a warren, a twisted tangle of streets and alleys and lanes. Though there are some grid-patterned streets where civic endeavor has in the past attempted some order, this enormous city is a comfortable rat's nest, the streets having grown as need and inclination directed. Opportunities to remake the city were resisted not only after the various Edo disasters, but after the 1923 earthquake and the 1945 fire-bombing as well.

The reason was, of course, that the warren was preferred. It was seen (better, felt) to be the proper human environment. The Japanese, like the English, prefer the cozy, and consequently the streets of Tokyo are as crooked and twisting as those of London.

There is a corresponding sense of belonging as well. The cozy warren is just for us, not for those outside.

Which is what one might expect from a people who make so much of what is private (ours) and so little of what is public (theirs). For such folk the neighborhood is of primary importance (and Tokyo is a collection of village-size neighborhoods), and its public aspect attains intimacy only when incorporated into the well-known.

For example, sections of old, twisted Tokyo are being torn down. Not because of any civic planning, but so that the most expensive land in the world may be more profitably used. And the new buildings are often built four-square, with straight streets. Not from any notions of urban efficiency, however; it is merely that buildings are most cheaply constructed if they are squarish and right-angled.

So, the old tangle is torn down. And it is rebuilt, incorporated within the basement of the high rise that took its place. There again are the bars, the little restaurants, the warren reborn.

The significance of public areas belonging to no one is not that they belong to everyone but that they can be used by just anyone. This means that the owners or lessees of private land in public places can be as idiosyncratic as they like.

Take modern Tokyo architecture. Visitors are astonished by its variety, given what they may have heard of the Japanese character. Instead of the expected conformity, they are presented with the wildest diversity.

The glass-and-concrete box (cosmetics) is next to the traditional tile-roofed restaurant (sukiyaki and *shabu-shabu*), which is next to a high-tech, open-girder construction (boutiques), which is next to a pastel-plastered French provincial farmhouse (designer clothes).

The architecturally odd is there to attract attention. Thus Tokyo mainstreet architecture has much the same function as the signs and banners that decorate it. To stand out is to sell something better. (As for conformity, there is plenty of that, but it is found in nothing so superficial as architecture.) Though profit may be a motive for eccentric architecture, it is not its only result. Among others, the stroller is presented with an extraordinary walking experience.

With space used in this distinctive fashion, one naturally wonders about the uses to which time is put. These are, as one might have expected, equally noteworthy. It is not so much that one can time-travel in Tokyo (and can do it even better in Kyoto), go from the seventeenth to the twentieth to the eighteenth century by walking around a block. One can, after all, do that in many European cities, which have more old buildings than Tokyo. Rather it is that Tokyo provides a fantastic rate of temporal change. In Europe a building was built for a century. In Tokyo a building, it often seems, is built but for a season.

They go up and come down at an almost alarming rate. In the Shinjuku and Ikebukuro sections, if you miss a month, you might well next time get lost, so fast and frequent are the metamorphoses. What you remembered has now become something else. And the hole in the street, the vacant lot, now holds the current architectural icon, a glittering chrome-and-glass structure like a giant lipstick or a mammoth lighter.

Old Edo had its construction-destruction compulsions as well, but they were different in that, first, there were so many fires that the reconstruction came to be seen as repair; and second, the new structures were not extreme because there were sumptuary laws and because the Edoite had only wood, tile and stone.

Now there are certainly no laws against display, and the Japanese architect has steel, glass, concrete and plastic, all of which can be forced into any shape desired.

The temporal dislocation in Tokyo is so extreme that the capital is, consequently, never finished. It is in a permanent state of construction. Like life it is always in flux. It is an illustration of itself — a metaphor for continual change.

The display of the Tokyo street, the Tokyo park, the Tokyo garden is thus a varied and a complicated thing. Walking becomes a variegated experience with many a surprise.

This is not perhaps unique to Tokyo, but is certainly not typical of the world's major cities. There — Washington, D.C., Beijing, Moscow — one is presented with a view and the view is the experience. Once you have glanced at it you have comprehended and no amount of strolling about will add anything. There is nothing left to discover after the view of the Capitol, the Temple of Heaven or the Kremlin.

Obviously, human variety was not in the minds of these architects; rather, it was human similarity that was being both courted and celebrated. And Tokyo, too, has its monolithic views — but it only has two of them: the Imperial Palace and the Diet Building.

Otherwise, there are no views at all. Everywhere you look it is a chaos, but what a fascinating chaos it is. It is a mosaic city, a melange city. It has no center. It has no outside. It even seems to lack the structural supports we know from other cities.

One of these we know from the early medieval city and from its modern descendant, the Islamic city. This is the division into trade towns. Streets of the goldsmiths, area of the camel drivers, pits of the dyers — that sort of thing. Such remains are visible in all major cities: the West Side of New York, for example.

Tokyo has something of this, things bunched together from the old days before there was public transportation: Otemachi, where the banks' headquarters are; Sudacho, where the wholesale cloth merchants are; Akihabara, down the street, where the cut-rate appliance people are.

But this grid cannot be used to comprehend the city because it is not operative. It is simply left over. Operative is a micro-grid that finds a bank, a cloth merchant, an appliance store in every neighborhood. And there are hundreds of neighborhoods in each district, and dozens of districts in each section, and tens of sections in this enormous city.

Duplication, therefore, becomes one of the features of a Tokyo walk. When you reach another public bath you are in a different neighborhood. And each neighborhood is a small town which has its laundromat, its egg store, its hairdressing parlor, its coffee shop.

Looking at the inner structure of Tokyo one is reminded of the inner structure of the traditional Japanese house. The sizes of the *tatami, fusuma* and *shoji* are invariable. The construction is by modular unit. City construction is likewise modular — the laundromat in Asakusa and the laundromat in Shinjuku are identical.

We of the West, used to large swaths of activity, do not know what to think of the filigree of Tokyo, its fine embroidery of human endeavor.

But we of the West know what to *feel*. Walking on the streets of Tokyo we are aware of a sense of human proportion that we might not have known in the city from whence we came. To walk in Tokyo is to wear a coat that fits exceptionally well.

The proportions (except where mania has taken over — the towers of west Shinjuku, for example) are all resolutely human. We raise our eyes to see buildings; we do not crane our necks. And the streets are narrow — all too narrow if it is one where cars are permitted. And there are little alleys just wide enough for a person. And there are things to look at.

Things to look at! Tokyo is a cornucopia held upside down. One does not know where to look first. If people say, and they do, that Tokyo makes them feel a child again, this is because it makes them all curiosity, all enthusiasm, all eyes.

This then is the display of Tokyo. It perhaps may be mercantile but its appeal goes far beyond the financial. Things become, in this plethora of sensation, detached from their utilitarian aspects. They exist for themselves: the cascades of kanji, the plastic food replicas in the restaurant windows, the façade, stories high, made entirely of TV sets.

One then remembers the woodcuts of Hokusai and Hiroshige — views of Edo — and sees the similarities. All of that detail, all of those particulars, all that decoration, the sheer movement of it — it is all real and it is all here now.

Especially on Sundays — the day (along with national holidays) when Tokyo turns itself again into Edo. The main streets in the major sections (Ginza, Shinjuku, Shibuya, Ikebukuro, Ueno) become malls. Motor traffic is forbidden (from 1 to 6 pm) and, as in olden times, people swarm into the streets. Unlike weekdays, when they rush about in the modern manner, on Sundays they stroll in the old-fashioned way. In Edo style they take their time, look at the stores, stop for a snack and saunter on.

Here, one thinks, looking at the leisured throng, Edo lives on. Despite the new backdrop of TV and computer games, the true human activity is the same, now as then. To leave the house and enjoy the display, to gaze at the latest and perhaps purchase a bit — this is what old Edo did and what new Tokyo does.

The new merchants, conservative as always, greatly feared for trade when the carless Sundays went into effect several years ago. They thought no one would come if they could not park their wheels. They were ruined, they wept in large advertisements. Not at all. They had not reckoned on the Edo spirit. Now the merchants look forward to Sunday and even department stores spill out onto the crowded streets. They have more customers on Sundays than they do on any other day of the week. Now smiling management gives out free balloons and plastic flowers to the passing crowd, while overhead kanji dances and neon glows in the sunlight.

All of Tokyo is out walking, sauntering through the streets, enjoying that amazing display which is Tokyo.

—1986

III

Gesture as Language

EVERYONE SPEAKS through gestures, but different countries have different gestures — or similar gestures with different meanings. Japan has a rich gesture vocabulary, but one which is not easily read by the foreigner, one indeed open to uninformed misinterpretation. At the same time, however, this language, once mastered, reveals or sustains a number of valid observations about the country.

A gesture, says Desmond Morris, is "any action that sends a visual signal to an onlooker." But what matters, he continues, "is not what we think we are sending out, but what signals are being received." Take, for example, the almost universal gesture of the circle made by thumb and forefinger. In America this means OK, based on an assumption that a circle is "perfect"; in France, however, the same gesture means just the opposite — the meaning is "worthless' because a circle is also a zero. And in Greece the gesture is an insult because it refers to an unmentionable, if circular, orifice in the body of the onlooker. In Japan, however, it means (coins being round) money.

The visiting American, Frenchman or Greek would all read this identical Japanese gesture "wrongly," with results which could be anything from amusing to disastrous. The signal sent out is not the signal received.

Japanese gestures are thus rich in opportunities for mistake. There is the famous example of the Japanese smile. The West had long been taught that the smile means pleasure, amusement or happiness. It is consequently there used accordingly.

But, as Lafcadio Hearn long ago observed, the Japanese smile is not only such spontaneous expression. It is also a form of etiquette and the Japanese child is still taught, usually through example, to smile as a social duty. Other countries, of course, also know of this usage, but there it is externalized and called the social-smile. In Japan the utility of the smile has been internalized. It has become, at least, a semi-conscious gesture and is to be observed even when the smiling person thinks he is unobserved. He races for the subway door, let us say. It closes in his face. His reaction to this disappointment is almost invariably a smile.

This smile does not mean happiness. No one is happy to have missed a subway. It does, however, mean cheerful acceptance. From an early age, the Japanese is taught to express no emotion which might disturb a sometimes precarious social harmony. Though scowls or even temper tantrums in the subway would not, in fact, upset society's equilibrium, this beautiful smile blooming in the teeth of disappointment does indicate that many taught gestures can become pseudo-involuntary, if social pressure is strong enough.

In Japan, indeed, this special gestural use of the smile can be extreme. Smiles at the death of a loved one are still to be witnessed. The message, properly read, is not that the dead are not mourned. Rather, the smiler is implying that bereft though I be, larger social concerns are more important and I am determined not to cause bother by making an emotional display upon this sad occasion.

Not all Japanese gestures, of course, bear this weight of social utility and hence this possibility for Western confusion. Some are just as confusing merely in their difference. For example, the presumably simple gesture of waving. We use it (palm open) to attract attention and (palm bent) to indicate farewell. The Japanese, however, use our "farewell" gesture to beckon. This gesture has become further confused in that, since World War II, the Japanese have also taken up waving goodbye. This they do by wagging the open palm sidewise — which is, of course, our gesture for getting attention.

Even those gestures which are identical in intent with those of the West always incorporate differences. Nearly universal, for example, is the right-handed gesture denoting the act of eating. The southern Italian for this is the bunched fingers of the right hand making a series of swift, lifting motions to the half-open mouth. The Japanese variation is two outstretched fingers making a circular motion in front of the closed lips. The Italian gesture mimes eating spaghetti, originally perhaps picked up with the fingers; the Japanese gesture mimics chopsticks. Both concern eating but if the Japanese does not know about pasta and the Italian has never seen *hashi* some cultural confusion is certain to occur.

Or, drinking. The same Italian raises his fist, throws back his head and sticks out his thumb. The Japanese lowers his head and makes a half-circle with thumb and index finger in front of his mouth, then suddenly tilts the whole hand. Here the European is imitating the act of drinking from a spouted wine-flask; the Japanese is miming drinking from a sake cup.

Nor do the difficulties end there. I, for one, am always confused by the Japanese eating gesture because I identify it with the smoking gesture — where two fingers are held in front of the mouth, the message usually reading "give me a cigarette." A yet further complication is that the old fashioned gesture for kissing is also two fingers held perpendicular to the lips. Did the occasion arise, I would be certain to mistake this for the give-me-a-cigarette or even the let's-eat gesture.

Simpler to read, but quite arcane enough for the first-time visitor, are the large number of professional imitative gestures. The carpenter mimes the actions of the saw, the barber imitates the scissors, the bartender the motions of the cocktail shaker. All of these happen to be identical with those of the West (except the carpenter's — the saw cuts when it is pushed rather than pulled) and are readable after a little practice. Not so easy to make out, however, are those imitative gestures indicating purely Japanese professions. The flower-arranger mimes an *ikebana* as he talks and the tea-master makes stirring motions. One must know what these represent in order to know what they mean. Fortunately they are coded. The barber always makes the same gestures, so does the tea master. If you can read one you can read them all.

Occasionally, however, for an unexpected profession, the gesture can prove baffling. In Sanya, in the slums of Tokyo, I repeatedly observed a very odd gesture — a rapid opening and closing of the hand. Upon investigation I discovered that this was a new entry into the professional imitative repertoire. It is a simple pumping motion (fist closed, then opened) and indicates that the gesturer has made some money by selling to the local blood bank.

Equally difficult for the uninformed are the various finger gestures. There the difficulty lies in that they rest upon a subcode which is assumed. To break this code one must realize that fingers are seen as, typically enough, a family system. The child is early taught that the thumb is the parent finger, specifically the father finger (*otosan-yubi*). The index is then the mother finger, the middle and ring fingers are elder/eldest brother/sister, and the littlest (*ko-yubi*) is his very own — often called the *boku* (me) *yubi*.

Perhaps all the fingers were at one time used for familial designation and its extensions but now only the thumb and little finger are used for visual signals. The little finger held in the air means, originally and primarily, a baby. Held aloft it traditionally asks if the couple has yet been blessed. The secondary, and now much more common meaning, however, is "girl-friend." I do not know how this transference took place but I do know that the little finger held up before your eyes on the street corner always asks if you are indeed waiting for "her." Likewise, the thumb has come to have a number of meanings, including "boy-friend." Most commonly, however, it retains its original parental attribute. It means father, master, employer, or — in the Japanese gang-world — the *oyabun,* boss.

Fingers are extensively used in the gesture vocabularies employed by Japanese gamblers and gangsters. Such, to be sure, are seen equally in all countries: members often wish to communicate in front of some third party but want to be neither overheard nor understood. A great many such gestures are thus international: crossed wrists means jail not only in Japan but in most countries as well. Probably only Japanese gangsters, however, understand the sharp pulling of the index fingers (as though shooting a gun) to mean pickpocketing, or the crossing of the index fingers (like swords) to indicate a fight.

The gesture vocabulary of gamblers is particularly rich. A rapid flicking of the thumb against the curved index finger is a reference to *pachinko,* that very popular form of pinball which is Japan's true national sport. Mahjong is indicated either by moving both arms as one does when mixing the tiles, or by imitating movements used when setting up a tile row. Dice-box gambling is indicated by a wave (side to side) of the hand, fingers loose. An interesting non-imitative gambling gesture is that used to indicate the card-game *hana-fuda*: the side of the nose is rubbed with the thumb. This is a visual pun. The game translates as "flower (*hana*) cards" but *hana* is also a homonym for "nose."

Another interesting gambler gesture, its origins somewhat obscure, is that for cheese-it-the-cops. This consists of hitting the forehead with the thumb end of the fist. Though the context in this case determines the message — resulting as it does in a general scampering — confusion is possible in that it is almost identical with another and more general gesture. The thumb end of the fist is shaken near the face to indicate that someone is *gatchiri* or *katai* with his money — both gesture and meaning being covered, in this case, by an identical English term: tight-fisted.

The fist is again used when something is suddenly remembered (usually with disastrous consequences) or suddenly understood (usually for the worse). Then the top of the speaker's own head is struck, often with the fist, though sometimes with the flat of the hand. The West has this self-punishing gesture, but it is always the temples which are slapped. The Japanese chastise the entire head.

The head is also used in a number of other ways indicative of a general lack of self approval. The painful scratching of the back of the head always means that the scratcher is embarrassed. (In America the same gesture means: I don't know.) It indicates, precisely, embarrassment coupled with unease — usually after a slip of some kind has occurred, or just after an ordeal (school speech, appearance on TV, etc.). One might think this as semi-involuntary as the smile, but its use seems more conscious. After all, in Japan being embarrassed is not only nothing to be ashamed of, it is a kind of social virtue, indicating as it does that one knows one's proper and subservient place. I have seen this gesture consciously used in order to create this kind of impression.

One major difference between Japanese and Western gestures, as seen in all of these examples, is that this rich manual vocabulary is almost never used, as it were, in the second-person singular. Questions may be asked, (little finger?/thumb?), but statements, in particular derogatory ones, are not to be made. Thus Japan has no second-person gestures so graphic as the Spanish biting of the thumb, the American thumbing of the nose, the Middle-European meaningful extension of the middle finger, the Italian thrust of the entire arm, stopped short by the other hand on the biceps.

Hand gestures as statement tend to refer either to self or to some third person not present. Following the custom of the spoken language (comments are made about "me, him, and her" but rarely about "you"), gestures are directed "away" from the watcher. Take, for example, the matter of making horns with the fingers. This is a universal sign occurring in many cultures where it has a number of meanings, all of them uncomplimentary.

In southern Europe, where it suggests cuckoldry, proven or not, the horns are often directed at the suspected victim himself. The perhaps primary European meaning, aversion of the evil eye, finds it — perforce — directed "against" the viewer. This second-person use never occurs in Japan though the "horns" (index and little fingers stiffly extended) mean things just as socially unacceptable: namely, jealousy or (secondary meaning) anger.

"My wife is always so (fingers make horns — reading: jealous) that I just hate to go home." Or: "Today my boss is (fingers make horns — reading: angry) and I'm not going to go near him." This usage is almost always referential to a third-person. I know of only one instance where this unpleasant gesture is used in a first-person context. This is when imps are invoked to torment misbehaving children. The finger-horns are "worn" by the irate adult who rushes directly at the offending child with loud cries of *oni! oni!*

There are several exceptions, however, to the general rule that in this land of harmony an overt second-person gesture is not permitted. These are the number of mild and/or amusing "statement" gestures specifically designed for second-person use. One is particularly charming. The speaker delicately scratches the space between the bottom of his nose and the top of his lip. This takes the place of the slightly improper phrase *hana no shita ga nagai*, though just why the length of this area should indicate the degree of the other's potency I have no idea.

This gesture, like most of the others already mentioned, are used by men with men. Japan joins the other nations of the world in excluding women from most of its gesture-making activities. For whatever reason (unrefined, unladylike, etc.), it is men who discourage women from thus expressing themselves. Of all the examples mentioned so far the only one I have seen women engage in is the oni demon-calling.

Women are, however, permitted (indeed, encouraged) to use a certain variety of gesture not unknown in other countries but perfected to a degree in Japan. It has a specifically "cooperative" intention, and often represents a request for a degree of social tolerance. One example, is that quite graceful gesture, half request, half expression of intent when, hand held carefully in front, one enters a row of seats or walks in front of another person. A full-scale version of this is seen when a person walks across the street just as the light is changing. There the hand is held high, like a flag, but it is also "humbly" bent at the elbow — a gesture which both requests and proclaims.

There are a vast number of "cooperative" gesture in Japan, but many of them are "negative." One might call them "absent" gestures except that they operate gesturely for positive results. In a crowded train or subway, for example, there is almost no eye contact among the passengers. Each studiously ignores the others. Here the gesture is the apparent lack of one. Or, a number of barrier signals are used — crossed arms if one is sitting, for example. Or, one moves further away (if possible) to maintain personal space, an area somewhat larger in size in over-crowded Japan than it is in wide-open America. While none of these are "gestures" they all serve as such. The most interesting thing about their use in Japan, (most of them being seen in other cultures as well) is the *way* in which they are used. They are rarely used "defensively," though defense is indeed their purpose. Instead, with everyone doing them, all in the same way, the effect becomes one of a greater cooperation, everyone doing what is expected and everyone doing so at the same time.

Such social "gestures" are extremely common in Japan as are those, some of which have already been noted, which are purely cooperative in intent. One of these is, of course, the famous Japanese bow. It is, strictly, a gesture meaning submissive behavior and is so used by many cultures. In Japan, however, the point of the bow is that its length and degree must (among social equals) be the same on both sides. One often sees polite gentlemen and genteel ladies glancing surreptitiously to gauge both the depth and the duration of the other's bow. Though the company president need only nod to the secretary's bow, confronted with an equal, he must not appear any less polite than his fellow bower. Submission turns into a kind of contest as to who is the more refined, and such bowings can go on for an amount of time.

What one might have misread as a mutual display of submission is then actually a cooperative leveling of differences, a removal of grounds for social disagreements, an assurance (however empty) that we are all alike and that we are mindful of the larger social concerns. At the same time one can see that bowing, like the Japanese smile (and like many of the other gestures mentioned here), can suggest a number of valid observations about this country where the direct second-person encounter is so avoided, where "face" is considered of vital importance, where gestural statements of intent take the form of requests, and where embarrassment is, indeed, nothing to be ashamed of.

—1980

Signs and Symbols

THE TRAVELER TO Japan soon notices a vast number of signs and symbols around him. These marks, figures, emblems, purveying information and displaying advertisements, crowd the cities and dominate the horizons. Signs seem to be everywhere—on roofs, walls, doors, and windows. Almost every available surface carries a message.

These messages the traveler has little hope of deciphering. If he could read them, he would probably pay them no more attention than he gives the plethora of signs and symbols in his own country. Since, however, he cannot read them, his attention is drawn to them all the more strongly.

They are obviously a functional part of the environment. They clearly proclaim. And they are often beautiful. The visitor admires the pleasing abstract shapes, the skill with which many are executed. His enjoyment of them is both primary and proper because traditionally signs and symbols in Japan are also meant to be aesthetically pleasing. Still, the illiterate visitor is missing a great deal.

To be sure, some signs are universal. Red is for negative directions, green for permissive, yellow for warning. This he understands, as well as the use of red to signify hot, and blue to show cold. Moreover, since Japan uses universal pictographs, he can tell which is the men's toilet or when he is approaching a railroad crossing. Most other messages, however, remain opaque, though to the Japanese around him the meaning is so transparent that they seem not even to notice.

If the visitor stays for a time he will begin to discriminate among the messages. Just as a child learns, he will start by sorting the signs into groups or classes, and the first class will probably be according to shape. Traffic signs, for example, are usually distinguished not only by a written message but also by shape. In America their form is standardized: stop signs are octagonal; yield signs are equilateral triangles with one point down; warning signs are diamond-shaped. Japan has an analagous shape vocabulary that one readily learns.

The next method of sorting the signs out is by location. In most countries, municipal information—"Don't walk," "Keep to the left"—is posted in a predetermined and logical place. Traditionally *all* information is this rigorously placed in Japan. Thus the Japanese restaurant has three positions where its name and sometimes its speciality are displayed—the signboard, the shop curtain and the lantern. Once in Japan, the foreigner soon learns to look in these places, but even then he often does not know what he is seeing. The reason is the language, the medium through which the message is conveyed.

The Japanese written language is a complex of ideograms and syllable signs covered broadly by the term *ji,* which means "letters." It is comprised of Chinese *(kanji),* and two syllabaries. The first syllabary, *hiragana,* is used for phonetic renderings of native Japanese words and the second, *katakana*, is usually for phonetic renderings of words transliterated from other languages.

A Chinese character usually represents a whole idea, and thus it is a complete word in itself, a system that reduces the need for sentence structure. In a country depending on an alphabet, a sentence, even if elliptical, is needed to convey a thought of any complexity. In kanji country it is the character itself that often stands for all, and is all that is necessary. Centuries of using this system have developed in people an extraordinary ability not only to read the characters themselves but also the nuances and overtones that surround and color each character.

We follow a somewhat similar process when, for example, we read "The Pause that Refreshes," and absorb its message without even thinking what the phrase means. It could be argued, however, that when the Japanese read the character 酒 (the kanji for sake), for example, associations of conviviality, warmth, solace and enjoyment emerge more strongly than when we read the word "whisky." Our word is a combination of alphabetic letters, like every other word we have, while the Chinese character stands more strongly for the thing itself. It represents it more directly than a word written with alphabetic letters can, and this helps account for the way the Japanese react to their signs. (Whether or not such an argument is valid, at least the Japanese themselves seem convinced of it.)

Just as the Japanese are alive to the nuances of the word itself, they are also aware of the way the word is written. In the West, unless you work in publishing or printing, you are no longer likely to be sensitive to the effects of different sytles of typography. We know the bold lettering of news headlines and the fanciful script of wedding invitations, but few others, and the fact that virtually all our communications are printed mechanically has blinded us to the infinitely subtler nuances of handwriting styles. In Japan, however, calligraphy is still an important aspect of life.

The effectiveness of any sign or symbol depends on the nexus of associations surrounding it. A symbol reminds us of all the attibutes we associate with what it represents. Even the simplest of symbols— ● or NO ENTRY — can carry fairly complicated associations, and much more is conveyed when the writing itself gives a resonance to the basic sense.

Again we can find an example in our own culture. If in America we come across 𝔜𝔢 𝔒𝔩𝔡𝔢 𝔈𝔫𝔤𝔩𝔦𝔰𝔥 𝔗𝔢𝔞𝔯𝔬𝔬𝔪𝔢, we know more than that food and drink are available. The message is grasped at once, for the lettering gives an indication of what kind of food and drink and what kind of ambience to expect. Both the affectations of Gothic script and of carefully obsolete spelling indicate gentility and respect for age. Certainly the atmosphere will be more contrived than in an establishment that simply proclaims EATS. There is also the implication that the clientele of such a tearoom will be older rather than younger, with more women than men. All these complicated overtones we take in at a glance. The full message is understood without our thinking about it. We receive the message the proprietors have directed at us. We have an instant index of the place.

In Japan the process is essentially similar. The reading and interpretation, however, allow for far more complicated judgments. The main reason for this is that there are many styles of script, each with its own associations.

To begin with, the Japanese distinguish among four major categories of written scripts. The first of these, *reisho*, evolved from China before the Han dynasty, and derives from the lettering used for inscriptions carved on stone or on seals. (There is another form as well, also stiffly Chinese, *tensho*.) The second, dating from late Han, is called *kaisho*. It is a calligraphic sytle from which the Japanese developed katakana. The third is *gyosho*, the style in which most Japanese write. The fourth style is the fluid *sosho*, from which came hiragana, or, as it was once called, *hentaigana*. It is so loose that it is often difficult to read and the Japanese say that anything more fluid than *sosho* is illegible. These styles will become clearer after examining the illustration below. The character is *tsuki*, or "moon," and this pronunciation is indicated phonetically in the hiragana printed forms. The pair of katakana (separated vertically by a dot) indicate two other pronunciations (and meanings) also carried by this character. First is *getsu*, as in *getsuyobi*, the word for "Monday." (We have something similar. We have "moon" and we also have a form of the word in Monday.) The second group of katakana indicates another meaning and pronunciation: *gatsu*, the suffix used in the months—*ichigatsu, nigatsu, sangatsu* (January, February, March), etc. This, then, is what the character means.

| Reisho | Kaisho | Gyosho | Sosho | Printed forms |

The various scripts, however, indicate or create nuances. To explain this, let us pretend that there are four restaurants, each calling itself Tsuki and using this character. What kind of atmosphere would you expect if each one used a different style of lettering?

To Japanese, the reisho character could only indicate a Chinese restaurant or else a place with very old associations, either authentic or assumed. The feeling might be a little like our Olde

Tearoome, China being to Japan as England is to America. The second place, with its name in kaisho script would not tell too much since this is the style widely used for many signs. The nuances might be understood as "traditional" or as "everyday." In either case there would be an association with Tokyo and the culture implied by the "new" capital.

With signs in gyosho or sosho, however, one's thoughts would turn to the old capital, Kyoto, and its softer, mellower moods. A shop sign in gyosho indicates a degree of refinement, a kind of delicacy that could be feminine. Sosho, which many Japanese find hard to read, can also indicate self-conscious elegance—perhaps something with an artistic flavor.

While all of this may seem recondite enough to the Westerner, it is only the beginning. Each of these styles has subdivisions. There is, for example, the script called *Edo-moji*. This category, associated with Tokyo during the eighteenth century, consists of styles named *kantei, yosei, joruri, kago,* and *kaku-moji*. From each of these come other styles. Kantei, for example, produced the *kabuki-moji*, a style associated mainly with that drama, and the *sumo* or *chikara-moji*, connected mainly with sumo wrestling. In addition, there is the popular Edo style called *hige* (or "whiskered")-*moji*, in which individual bristle strokes are visible. A cursive script, near gyosho in feeling, the "whiskered" *moji*, though intended to be spontaneous and free, is, in fact, rigidly stylized. The passage of the brush must leave seven distinct bristle marks; in the narrower parts of the character it must show five, and as it leaves the paper it must show three. This seven-five-three formula, derived from China, is an auspicious combination applied to many occasions, such as the shrine visits of young children at these three ages.

Again, all of this is arcane to Westerners—and, it might be added, is becoming remote to Japanese as well. Yet there is still a wealth of nuance, a treasury of shared and accepted associations that all Japanese derive from their signs and symbols.

The process is less complicated than it sounds, because no conscious thought is involved in this kind of reading. Such nuances are felt at once or not felt at all. Since associations are involved—"feelings" rather than "thoughts"—putting them into words makes them sound more rigid and definitive than they are.

Japan's proliferation of signs and symbols consists overwhelmingly of commercial advertising. And the viewing audience is not only the potential paying customer but also the neighbors, the interested, the uninterested, the whole society, and (if we consider votive tablets) the gods themselves. Advertising in Japan is a public art and a cultural force.

Underlying this art of advertising is the more basic art of calligraphy. Whether the medium is black ink or neon tubing, the aesthetics of calligraphy can move foreigners almost as deeply as Japanese. It is the beauty of the forms as much as their meaning that is appreciated. Among Japanese, an individual is still judged by the way he forms his characters. Letters from strangers are read not only for what they say but also for the way they are written. Bad writing still means a bad, or at least weak, personality. Since the Japanese typewriter remains at best a cumbersome affair and is, at any rate, never used for personal correspondence, a good, clean, even elegant hand is a requisite. Aesthetic qualifications become moral qualifications in Japan; beauty becomes honesty. How all this will fare in the era of the home word-processor remains to be seen.

—1974

A Vocabulary of Taste

SOME YEARS BACK an attempt was made to introduce the Japanese aesthetic term *shibui* into American advertising parlance. There was a shibui dress design, a shibui look to your guest room, and a shibui necktie. Such are, I suppose, possible, but only if you know what you are doing. The perpetrators did not. Last heard of, shibui had taken its noun-form, *shibumi*, and become the title of a popular novel which had nothing to do with any of the qualities its title evoked.

This is too bad, because America needs words for such concepts. Having the word one could then enjoy the concept. Actually, shibui means astringent, but pleasantly so, like a persimmon or a lemon. An extension is that the shibui is sober but elegant, plain but distinctive. A shibui kimono, for example, is of a single color with just the hint of a contrasting shade — a blackish-greenish garment perhaps, lined with a coral silk barely visible at neckline and sleeve. This being so, the dictionary gives one final definition: "severe good taste," whether evidenced in dress, house, or garden — the kind of good taste we call quiet but distinctive.

How handy this term in English would be — just one word for all those many. Its failure to enter the language was no fault of its own. It was simply never properly defined.

In thinking over this failure, and the language's continued need, I wondered if, properly defined, several other convenient Japanese aesthetic terms could not after all weather the change and enrich the American language.

If so, I would first nominate *jimi*. The dictionary is of one mind about this term: it is "plain, simple, quiet, modest, unpretentious, sober.'' One sees its differences from shibui. Jimi can never be elegant, but it can be a number of other things. Yet what but jimi was the gray flannel suit, were those plain blouses and skirts that used to be considered so pleasantly unexceptional?

But, perhaps jimi's time on the American scene is already past — the unexceptional seems to play small part in what American exceptionals call their lifestyles. If such be the case, I have then the perfect now and with-it aesthetic term.

This, the antonym of jimi, is *hadé*. Here, even the dictionary lets itself go. It is "showy, gaudy, vain, flashy, gorgeous," obviously just the term for American lifestyles. What the dictionary does not indicate, however, is its most precious property: hadé is not pejorative, as are its English synonyms. It is, in Japan, possible to be loud without being vulgar. A hadé kimono can be alive with clashing color, yet perfectly proper. A personality can be equally hadé — outgoing, bright, flashy, even outrageous, but with no hint of opprobrium. America needs a term such as this.

Continuing on, encouraged, one encounters the celebrated and infamous twins of Japanese terms aesthetic. These are *sabi* and *wabi*: celebrated because indispensable; infamous because of their being so notoriously difficult to define.

Here even the dictionary is uncertain. Both are rooted in words that mean "lonely" (*sabishi* and *wabishi*, respectively), but this is of small aesthetic assistance. Perhaps a history lesson will help.

It will be remembered that in the West, in the very midst of sentimental rococo excesses, the new classicism made its entrance. This occurred in many European countries and not for the first time. When things get just too frivolous a new sobriety comes into being.

This occurred earlier in Japan. The warlord Hideyoshi was con-
structing tea-ceremony rooms of pure gold. The temperature of
the times was nothing if not hadé. It was Hideyoshi's arbiter on
matters aesthetic, Sen no Rikyu, who took matters in hand and
popularized a new sobriety, in which wabi and sabi played a large
part.

A paradigm for the new attitude was Hideyoshi's visit to see
Rikyu's celebrated garden of morning glories. When he arrived
he discovered that they had all been uprooted. The disgruntled
warrior repaired to the tea-room. There, in the alcove, in a common clay container, was one perfect morning glory.

How the ruler reacted to this lesson — less means more — is
not recorded. Fulsomely chronicled is the general reaction: the
new sobriety became the latest thing. Blossoms common as weeds
were put in peasant pickled-plum pots and the *wabi-cha* style of
ikebana was formed. Backed by a scroll consisting of lots of white
space and a few perfectly placed lines, the result was terribly sabi.
One is quite reminded of Marie Antoinette's Hameau with its real
hay and real cows.

There was a catch, of course — there always is in Japanese
aesthetics. These common little bowls, perhaps cheap enough at
first, soon came to be — crafted by the most sensitive of potters
— more expensive than anything Hideyoshi could have commis-
sioned. The ostentatiousness of the unostentatious became the major sabi/wabi theme, and it still is. The West, sunk in frivolity,
knows all about this, but it does not yet have a name for it. It
yearns for the new sobriety but does not know what to call it.
Here is where sabi/wabi are desperately needed. What, indeed,
are designer jeans if not sabi — that pleasant combination of the

old, the sturdy, the proletariat, upgraded by expensive hands into the most unostentatiously ostentatious of objects? And, as for wabi, my nomination is Chanel's simple, basic, black frock. It is common but elegantly cut, in the most unexceptionable of colors, but the single one forever in fashion; it speaks of a lonely independence, and is inordinately expensive.

Sitting in one's Chanel, gazing at an arrangement of dandelions in a piece of battered Tupperware, one may now practice (the last term in today's lesson) *mono no aware*. This is not an attribute but an attitude — one, naturally, with a long and involved history.

For American purposes, however, it is sufficient to note that, in *The Tale of Genji* and before, its use signalizes a (dictionary term) "sensitivity to things," the things themselves being "things which move one." The awareness is highly self-conscious and what moves one is, in part, the awareness of being moved, and the mundane quality of the things doing the moving. Here we are again close to wabi because it is the spectacle of quotidian life itself that comprises the view. The mutability of all things, their transience — life is a stream down which one glides and this is both pleasantly melancholy and, at the same time, terribly human. Mono no aware implies resignation but, at the same time, it occasions a small celebration of this attitude. And here is where America's need for such a term occurs. You look into the mirror and find one more line, one more gray hair. Mono no aware does *not* consist of picking up the phone and making an appointment at the beauty parlor. Rather, it consists of smiling gently at one's reflection and thinking: "Ah, mono no aware. Things are going as they must . . . and therefore should."

If America has this real need for Japanese autos, transistors,

computers, and it seems it does, how much more real its need for
Japanese aesthetic terms to really define how it is feeling.

—1983

The Tongue of Fashion

ONE EXPRESSES oneself in various ways: deeds, words, gestures. The expression is presentational: one shows who one is, or who one wishes to be taken for, by the choice of word or gesture. There are many systems of expression, some well known, some known scarcely at all. Spoken and written language, for example, is a very well studied system of expression: the weight and nuance of each word, of each grammatical construction is known. This knowledge is consciously applied when one writes or speaks; one creates the impression of who one hopefully is through a choice among its many parts. Other forms of expression are scarcely studied at all, though used none the less. Various kinds of gesture, in themselves forming languages, have been only partially codified, and among these clothing as a system of expressing feeling and thought is rarely studied at all. Yet, as a means of self-comment and self-presentation it is one of the most common forms of gestural language: the ''sentence'' formed by the complete ensemble speaks plainly about the wearer and is so intended to; the language is well understood though rarely (Roland Barthes is an exception) acknowledged.

In Japan, a land where the emblematic is most visible and where signs and signals are more openly displayed, the language of dress is more codified than in many countries in the West. It is consequently better known and more consciously used. Kunio Yanagida, the early folklorist has said (as quoted by Bernard Rudofsky) that ''clothing . . . is the most direct indication of a people's general frame of mind.'' This observation is shared by a

majority of Japanese — or at any rate used to be when the traditional Japanese costume was their only form of sartorial expression. It said much about the country and the people and indeed
did express their general frame of mind.

The kimono comes in only two sizes, male and female. It is also
never designed to fit the wearer. Rather the wearer is designed, as
it were, to fit *it*. The assumption is that we Japanese are all alike
(except for the important sex difference, about which too much
cannot be made) and, this being so, tailoring as a form of unique-
ness is not valued in this land where the truly unique is so often
unwelcome. Since harmony is our goal in all things we show our
happy similarity in our national costume.

To be sure there is room for minor variation. A young girl
shows she is young by wearing bright kimono; an old women
shows she is old by wearing only subdued colors. Traditionally
the wealthy but otherwise unpriviledged merchant class indicated
their state by plain kimono lined with the most expensive
materials. Both kimono pattern and hair style indicated the social
position of the wearer — a geisha would "look" quite different
from the married woman of good family.

The kimono, like all forms of dress, also shows much more
than it ostensibly presents. The language of clothes, like any other
language, is filled with nuance and deeper meaning. The kimono
defines the wearer in more senses than one. Though not shaped to
the body, it encircles and confines the body, it holds and supports
it, as do few other forms of dress.

In contrast to the Arab kaftan or the Persian chador, which has
no contact with the body at all and only covers it, the kimono

delineates the wearer. It is, particularly in the woman's costume, so tight and so supported by layers of inner kimono, that it is like a moulded shell.

What is moulded, however, are not the breasts, the hips, the behind, those areas emphasized in the West, but the human form itself, the torso. The result is a costume so tight that it hobbles the wearer and prevents any actions other than walking, standing, sitting, kneeling, a repertoire of movements which, given the possibilities of the human body, is quite limited. The inescapable suggestion is that something this tight and constricting must therefore enclose — like the lobster's shell — something soft and fluid.

In this sense the kimono can be seen as a metaphor for the idea that the Japanese has of himself — and is hence presenting. We are a people whose social consciousness is at least as strong as our individual consciousness; we live in a rigid conforming society and both our strong social self and the strong social rules we obey are necessary because we would otherwise not know who we were. Like the lobster we are defined not by an inner core but by an outward armor — which may be social or sartorial. These — our ideas, our clothes — are informed from the outside. We so express our social self because, to an extent, that is all there is.

At the same time, however, the social contract has many escape clauses and the kimono itself has myriad possibilities for individual variation. Our emotions, our vagrant fears and wishes, can all be expressed so long as we show these only within the context of our society and its laws; this is visible within the context of the kimono, our national costume, the Japanese dress.

A standard costume is like an accepted idea. It is self-evident.

One does not examine its meaning until one has ceased to believe in it. In the same way, the meaning of the kimono was not apparent until it stopped being widely worn. Now we see that — a truism — those who wear kimono also entertain old-fashioned ideas. At the same time there lingers, naturally enough, an air of the respectable about the kimono. The well-brought-up girl has one and wears it upon the proper occasions (weddings, tea-ceremony lessons, New Year's) though the rest of the time she may be in jeans. She is showing that she is a decent girl but that she also has modern ideas. She is not suggesting, I think (which would be the suggestion of the American girl gotten up for an American wedding), that she is just wearing the garment for peripheral reasons but that the real her is different. Rather she is stating that she is both modern and respectable at the same time.

Hers is one solution (sometimes in kimono, sometimes in jeans) to a communicative problem which the Japanese have been facing for some time now. How do you indicate sartorially who you are when the vehicle for so doing is disappearing. And particularly when there is a strong taboo against — a possible answer — wearing Japanese and Western costume in combination.

When Japan began modernizing itself a hundred years ago many were the mistakes — bustles worn backwards and the like. More important, the Japanese were not prepared to read properly the lexicon of Western dress. As might have been expected the Japanese choice was initially for Western clothing too formal for either the occasion or the person or both. Hats, gloves, sticks — elements known to have had originally aristocratic nuances — were used by all Japanese men who could afford them. The women likewise were always too dressed up. One still sees remnants of this early reading in even informal court functions and the Japanese abroad are usually, given foreign standards, over-dressed. That Japanese in Western clothes look always off to a wedding or a funeral is an old observation but one still, to an extent, valid.

One can understand the reasons. The rigidity of the kimono was being sought for in the rigidity of foreign formal dress. Over-dressing for an occasion, which is what all formal dress consists of, means by definition a presentation of the social self. The clothing is much like the conversation on such occasions — social, that is, impersonal.

The language of dress in the West is now nothing if not per-sonal and fashion has become a system of dialects. Individuality is sought for, if not always achieved, and social dress — as in formal dress — has all but disappeared. The Japanese, having scrapped their own native costume and having proved understandably maladroit in handling the various nuances of Western formal dress, are now presented with a new problem — or rather, the same old problem in a new guise: how to present the social self given only the apparently highly individualized clothing styles they are given a choice among.

To an extent the modern Japanese has the choice made for him by fashion itself, the linguistic equivalent of which might be free speech but the true aim of which is to make everyone for a season speak alike. The Japanese problem, its quest for clothing express-ing a social norm, is solved so long as everyone appears more or less the same, even though the clothing itself may have originally carried highly personal nuances.

Take jeans, for example. These have now become the uniform

of the young in all countries. Being a uniform this means that the young are all saying the same thing. Though the fashion (as fashion) was originally radical in America (we are not going to dress up, we are going back to the earth, we are egalitarian, etc.) and even to an extent revolutionary (down with formal clothing, down with elitist thought, down with civilization), it has now become the equivalent of an accepted idea and is defended only in that jeans are cheap, easy to wash, do not need pressing, and everyone else wears them.

In Japan jeans at once became a uniform for the young and originally carried the same message of youthful revolt, of attacking bourgeois ideas of respectability, of "thinking young." In no time, however, jeans (always chosen a size too small and given to shrinkage besides) became the kimono equivalent. They encase snugly and safely, and their message has become socially conciliatory — if everyone says the same thing, then no one says anything. Jeans became the unexceptionable container for young bodies, was accepted as such and its original somewhat inflammatory message has now become its opposite: we are conforming, we are rocking no boats.

Not that this has not occurred in other countries. And not that other countries do not likewise seek the safety and security of the unexceptionable social costume. My point would be that, in this as in other things, the phenomenon is more visible in Japan. And that, given the admitted difficulties the Japanese encounter in "reading" modern fashion, their mistakes are often instructive.

Take for example the emblazoned tee-shirt. In America, where the fashion first started, wearing a Coca-Cola tee-shirt, meant precisely that one would not subscribe to those institutionalized habits or virtues which accompany indiscriminate and habitual Coca-Cola drinking. The intent was ironic, as in so much American fashion. If one wore a Yale or a Harvard tee-shirt, not only did one not go to those schools but one also was expressing an ironic scorn for the qualities they presumably inculcate. Wearing surplus U.S. Army gear meant you were anti-Vietnam-War and hence anti-Army. Often the irony was a put down — the various confrontation messages worn across the chest — some witty, some not.

In Japan, however, Coca-Cola wearers love Coca-Cola. It is a sign of their modernity. The boy with Yale or Harvard on his chest would really like to attend these universities. To be this cosmopolitan is to be progressive. Surplus Army uniforms (always U.S., never Japanese) mean merely being with-it in some obscure (to the Japanese) sense. And as for the emblazoned messages, since no one can read them or, if reading them, understand them, the mere fact that one is wearing English on the tee-shirt indicates a contemporary and progressive frame of mind. Some of the results are startling. IF IT MOVES SUCK IT may be fitting on a sardonic American college boy but it is not (where I saw it) when it covers the bosom of an innocent Japanese highschool girl. The mock come-on or put-down built into the American youth context is entirely missing.

Yet, with it all, even when the ostensible message is not apprehended, the under-message (we are with it, we are among the new knowledgeables) is there. Printed tee-shirts everywhere mean I'm OK, you're OK. In Japan the printed foreign word (divorced of all meaning though it must be) is fashionable. One is not an old fogy, nor is one stuck in the mud. Rather, one is young, mobile, hopeful, and looking to further horizons. One is also cultured. Foreign words — English in Japan right now — have the same *éclat* that French in the menu used to have in America. The under-message is the same: we are cosmopolitan. This is important on a small, overcrowded, intensely provincial archipelago.

And sometimes the messages also coincide to a surprising degree in the two countries. Take, for example, the too-big look, clothes purposely several sizes too large, pants or skirt bunched at the belt, coat or blouse sleeves extending down over the hands, shoulders sagging because too wide — a brief fashion.

In America and Europe the message was that the girl in the too-large man's suit (and the fashion was male clothing on girls, though it consisted of not just any old men's suit but men's suits purposely designed too large for girls) was really saying that try as she may for a man's role in this man's world (now that she has been "liberated" enough to attempt it) the role is just "too big" for her.

This message may have had some slight relevance in America where there has indeed been an amount of publicity concerning women's presumed liberation, but in Japan where woman is not in the slightest liberated, the message, though presented, has no social relevance. It is a message without a context.

In America the implication was that the woman wearing this outfit and so obviously "failing" to perform the male role was, therefore, a figure of some fun. At the same time, she was attractive, as only a person who admits her faults can be attractive. She was "smart," "cool," "cute" — there are various adjectives incorporating several degrees of honesty and charm. She was also safe since she had nothing of the threat of the Womans' Libber about her — she was, in fact, a turn-coat, snuggling up to and affirming the male image.

In Japan all of this wealth of nuance is lost. The too-big look as a foreign fashion has simply been taken over unexamined. Japan has, however, also enlarged this particular fashion — and here is where the messages in the two countries coincide. Too-big costumes are also made for men — or, at least, boys. One sees these adolescents in the bunched and baggy trousers, the sagging coats which we in the West only associated with fashionable girls. Here then, the original American message, makes sense. Japanese male youngsters cannot "fill father's pants;" both the costume and social responsibilities it suggests in its original form are "too much" for the wearer. This large outfit is, tellingly, nothing other than the "grey flannel" suit long associated with an orderly and conservative life. There is no hippy costume which is "too big" and in Japan the idea of a kimono "too large" would no longer carry any meaning at all. The outsize ensemble (again especially tailored, usually in "natural" colors since natural, that is, earth colors are at present also fashionable — true legacy from the hippies) is a parody of Papa's best suit and means that Sonny cannot and will not live up to inherited responsibilities. Here the effect is consciously "funny," and young men so dressed are figures of fun (just as women in the West so dressed were — though in both countries "funny" is read as "charming" or "disarming" in that, like all joke outfits, this one really sets out to placate) because the context is understood. In Japan, boys so signally failing to live up to inherited virtues (hard work, the rat race, wife and family) cast some slight doubt on such virtues and since the doubt is there, the costume has a meaning. In the case of

girls wearing the same costume, however, the effect is meaningless. She is simply — neuter term — "fashionable."

If sometimes the messages of fashion coincide in both the West
and in Japan, most often they do not. Take, for example, the
American ensemble which consisted of the highly unfashionable:
materials such as georgette and velveteen cut in a deliberately old
fashioned manner — (puffed-sleeves, yoke neck) — and often accompanied by hair in a bun, or a primped permanent, and
sometimes granny-glasses. The message is that we are so serious
we do not care for fashion (though this ensemble, in fact, became
rapidly fashionable — a logical development from the earlier
"ugly-is-beautiful" fashion), and we in our own way care for and
have indeed found the true virtues — those of our grandparents
and not our parents. Further, we are sober and recognize true-
worth and are honest enough to proclaim this.

Such a complicated sartorial metaphor is not legible in Japan
where, in any event, the different strata of historical costume in
the West are not recognized. At the same time, since fashion is
fashion, this look is everywhere in the larger cities. Here, again,
however, some changes have been made. Since Japan has never
had a fashion which has been downgraded (and, as we have seen,
even the kimono is at certain times and places proper and hence
fashionable still), there is no need for irony. The Japanese see the
unfashionable look therefore as a continuation for one of their
own fashions: the velveteen and beribboned little-girl dress which
has, indeed, never gone out of fashion. Styles of the 'Thirties (to
which the American ensemble is most beholden) are not recognized as such and, in any event, the implied nostalgia cannot be felt.
Therefore, the American unfashionable look is treated as a logical

extension of Japan's own little-girl look. This says that I am innocent and nubile, of good family and am aware of my own
cuteness; I am something for you to admire and think fondly of.
Consequently granny glasses and puff sleeves as a fashion fit well
with ankle-length party skirts and hair ribbons. Kate Greenaway
is laid directly on top of Clyde's Bonnie.

Not only do the Japanese read Western fashion differently
(jeans), creatively (the too-big suit on the boy), and wrongly (the
ugly look), they are also not at all ''at home'' with it and never
have been. The only Western dress to which they have
thoroughly accustomed themselves and which they wear naturally
is the institutionalized costume.

We foreigners are used to this only in specialized professions —
nurses, stewardess, etc., and typically the wearers are usually
female. In Japan, however, the institutional costume is
everywhere. All Japanese cooks wear a ''cook suit,'' all white and
with a big puffed hat; most younger Japanese students wear the
black serge high-collar Prussian schoolboy suit; day-laborers con-
coct typical and usually identical outfits; even the ordinary man
off for a day of skiing or hiking fits himself out in a full skiing or
hiking ensemble. The conclusion is inescapable: the Japanese is
truly at home in Western dress only if it is some form of livery.

Allison Lurie has written that to wear livery is to be
''editorialized or censored,'' which is quite true. But it is also to
be — finally — defined. It is this, the need for this definition (at
the cost of editorialization and censorship, to be sure), which is so
felt by modern Japanese. One cannot wear jeans forever and so the
logical progress is therefore into identical dark business suits, with
white shirts and sober neckties, and company badges in the lapels.

To be defined is (in Japanese terms) to know who you are socially, or even sociologically. This is of prime importance. Thus, everyone "says" the same thing, and this "conversation" uses only the safest of clichés. If "who I am" is the sartorial message the world over, then clothes can also answer the even more pressing question of "who am I?" The Japanese response to this is: I am what I appear to be; I am the role and the function I am dressed for.

There are thus within the purely Japanese context no problems of ambiguity, dishonesty, irony, or intention vs. interpretation (terms Allison Lurie used in speaking of a possible vocabulary for dress). Likewise, since the costume which even the young must eventually opt for is so unequivocal, there is no room for eloquence, wit, or even any but the most rudimentary information. Unexampled similarity remains the ideal of Japanese dress — though the unavailability of the kimono, that most strictly Japanese of garments, is still obviously felt.

—1981

IV

Notes on the Noh

IT IS NOT IMPOSSIBLE to read the Noh as literature, but it is difficult. It requires the kind of imagination essential to anyone who sits in complete silence and reads a score. It also requires a like amount of skill — whether the text is translated or not. Going to the Noh in Japan is very like going to a chamber music recital elsewhere. Many have the text open in their laps. Since the language is so obscure, the delivery so slow, the syllables so drawn-out, most Japanese could not otherwise understand much. Even with the text, as with the score of a Schoenberg quartet, one must study it both before and after performance for the subtleties to become apparent. The pleasure lies in tracing the allusions, in understanding apparent ambiguities, in discovering the richness of the associations.

The text of Noh is a collection of poems, some by the author of the play, some not; it is a repository of popular songs of the day; language and often action turn on the pun, the pillow-word, the invented portmanteaux, pivot-words, conceits. Reading Noh is like reading late Joyce, like reading St. John Perse, like reading Webern. Each note, each word must be savored, weighed, calculated, and then put again into context; the context and never the word alone creating the image. Noh defies translation, as Chinese poetry, as Donne defy translation. Properly, Noh should include two pages of commentary for every two lines of text. When Hagoromo dances for her robe and sings of the heavens, she does much more than just this. What we are given is a created cosmography in which float bits of T'ang poetry, pieces of earlier Japanese, traditional refrains, and transient songs of the day. The language turns, convolutes, rears back upon itself. A near approach is Middleton, Webster, Ford; or, in Shakespeare, the echoing poetry of *Measure for Measure*, the subjective rant, all association, of Thersites in *Troilus*. The language of Noh is like music of the Elizabethan period, like the parade of reminiscences — controlled but seeming not — in the *Cries of London;* like the drinking-rounds and canons, cunning and lapidary. The Noh is mannerist drama.

The Noh text is concerned with the drama itself, with its description. Since bare action is as important to Noh as the bare stage, there are no jeweled stanzas, no encrusted couplets. A line may have five ambiguities but will contain not one metaphor. Instead, the scene is laid by adjectives, strings of adjectives, and we recognize the style — it is that of Greek poetry. The "autumn-winded pine-tree" and the "wine-dark sea" have a common ancestry. Both are nature poetry. In Noh, natural forces, natural surroundings, are everything — it is an animistic theater, the theater of pure Shinto. Demons come from rocks and ogres from trees, the angel descends from a pine, and the stage is peopled by the dead.

Nature is there not only in the images of the language but in other images as well. The backing of the stage is a single great pine, always the same yet always new, as constant as a ground-bass of Purcell, but equally varied as the chorus over it embroiders the scene. The costume is always a kimono but such a kimono as never walked the earth. Of indeterminate period, a synthesized garment, it is a landscape within itself. It is pure spider web, rich earth brown and silver skeins; it is autumn incarnate, red, orange, with a touch of dying green; it is a flaming maple tree or the spring's young cherry-blossom. The costume is a vista made animate and each slow turn, each upraised arm, reveal new views. The simple props of Noh — the fan, the rosary, the stool, the traveling hat, the skeleton of boat or temple — are indications. The costumes of the Noh are the images of the play itself. And the talk is of clothes: kimono sleeves get wet, trains trail, clasps open, obis slide; hats, hair, head-dresses, all are reflected in the text itself.

The Noh stage is a square raised platform and the audience is at the front and right. Like the reconstructed Elizabethan stage, like the boxing ring, it is a viewing platform. It is the plateau which holds the action, toward which, as though toward a target, all attention is directed. This is as it should be because Noh, like the Elizabethan theater and unlike ours, is a theater of action.

To read the Noh is to think of drama; to see it is to think of ballet — and it was those first seeing it who called it the "dance-drama of Japan." The costumes are theatrical in a way we have lost but for the dance; the movements are a ritual the like of which we retain only in ballet. The careful, creeping movements, heel-toe; the abrupt wheelings on the stage; the stamps; the sudden fallings on the knees — these we would call dance though what the Noh calls dance is more purely formal, a *numéro* embedded in the text, accompanied by the chorus, and rendered in English only by the stage direction: "she dances."

And this translation must suffice for that moment when the forces of the play are drawn into a knot, that incandescent moment when words no longer serve, when action must break the history, the story, the plot. The kneeling second actor — a classical fall-guy — has asked all the questions. The standing first

— facing the audience, masked, once human but now monster, demon, angel, thing — has answered every one. The final question — and the dance. She — he, it — will now show, will now demonstrate, will now repeat the action, as in that moment in therapy when the patient realizes he must live again, and this time live through, the forgotten, the refused, the evaded experience. At one remove, no longer what she was, faced with the absolute — that peopled world outside the stage — she lifts one foot, then the other, turns and the final revelation has begun.

A long, drawn-out, hour-long accelerando, ending in the incandescence of dance; a gradual, almost imperceptible movement from molto largo to prestissimo: this is the tempo of the Noh. To try and watch the tempo grow is like trying to watch the hour hand of the clock move, like trying to watch flowers open. Yet there are seconds when you realize that before your eyes this tempo has changed. It seems faster, you think. It really does. Then: It *is* faster. Then: It is much faster than I had thought. Midway through most Noh the tempo catches you, and what had seemed a uniform (dignified, serene, moving, leaden, dull, boring) flow is now revealed — after it is accomplished — as an incredibly subtle metamorphosis from dead stop to as fast as possile. And, at the height, somewhere past the middle of the play, comes the dance, the roaring, swooping, pounding, crushing dance of the demon or the ogre, the ecstasies of the mad ghost, nature for the first time appearing as typhoon, as earthquake, as terror and conflagration; or the quick dance of sorrow or bereavement, the dance of the mad, the spirit, the dead.

And this dance, the heart of danced Noh, occurs — when it occurs — always and precisely at the moment when truth is recognized, when shame is thrown off, when the first actor finally appears as he really is.

The opening of the Noh is on the level of our theater, it is slower but it is naturalistic. We are in a mountain pass, or in a forest, or by a sea-shore. The second actor — as truly our representative as ever was audience in *Knight of the Burning Pestle* — comes forward and speaks our language: I am called so-and-so; I come from such-and-such; I am here to tell you a story. Him we recognize; he is one of us. Then out comes a being who looks like one of us but is not. This we know from the mask, from the walk, from the unbelievable beauty of the landscape on his back. This is not one of us and the story of the play tells why. He walks, he talks, he tells his history, or a part of it. Questions are asked. They are partially answered, or they are evaded, or they are cunningly answered, with ambivalence, with double meaning. We circle warily around the truth. We guess but dare not ask.

Then the being disappears (the actor changes robes — into one even more magnificent), we and the second-actor both ponder, or in the old days were at this point distracted by a comic interlude, like the 19th century audience receiving a tidbit, a restorative in the shape of a delicacy by Hummel between the movements of a grand symphony by Spohr or Cherubini. Then the being reappears. It no longer creeps upon the stage. It strides with little steps. It races with almost no movement at all. It looms and swings its arms though its kimono sleeves are still. We are confronted. It was a ghost . . . it was an ogre . . . it was the spirit of a mother searching for her child . . . it was a soldier killed in his prime a hundred years before. It is what it is and nothing more. Words fail us, and it — the supernatural — no longer speaks. The dance begins.

Though the text is written, the music is not. It has been transcribed by patient scholars but this is not the same. The score is noted but lies in the memory of the performers. It is said to be always identical and, given the Japanese, their reverence, their fear, it probably is — with changes so minute that now one's great-grandfather would be reassured though Zeami find it unrecognizable.

It is a music of richness and complication. Like all music of Japan, it is not, however, absolute. It does not and cannot exist by itself. There are no suites from *Shunkan*, no symphonic-fragments from *Kumasaka*. The songs may be abstracted, studied and performed, but only if the text is retained complete. The music exists to punctuate the words. A dry, percussive music, it is extended *secco recitativo*, and musically of no more interest than that. But, in the context of the play, just as dance carries action, so music carries the words. Though at first all seems arbitrary, chaos is shortly vanquished, and form emerges. Amid the taps and clicks of hand-held drums, the banging of the floor-drum, the grunts and groans of chorus and musicians, the flute, a single voice that sings throughout, sustains emotion. Its skirlings, over-blowings, filigree, become the dance.

Music is to Noh what Wagner had in mind, but a Wagner unspoiled, without paraphernalia, without *leit-motiv*, without those bass cymbals which sound only twice during the four-evening performance. It is very near the world of *Pelléas*, and Debussy's instinct was sound because reading Noh is like reading

Maeterlinck. Just as the oboe becomes Mélisande, so the Noh flute is the voice of the first-actor when that actor no longer speaks.

The drums thump on, their sound and that of the stamping actor all confused, the sound of earth, the sound of man, the sound of death. And over it, amid the waving and kimonoed arms, like a bird let loose and circling, the flute spirals upward with the dance. It is the voice of the angel, the voice of the demon too. It is the sound of heaven, of any after life; it is the sound of truth disclosed.

The costume transfigures; the mask substitutes. Its function is seen in the fact that the second-actor wears none. There is no need. He has a face, he is human, he is alive. But not the first-actor — though the opening mask, the mask of the first half, may fool us, it looks so real. As in those moments of emotion when the mask bends down and we seem to see it weep, when the mask turns up and we seem to see it smile. It seems to move, this mask, and counterfeit our nature, but we know which face is real. It is that of the second-actor, who kneels by the side of the pillar and attempts to turn this face into a mask: no smiles, no frowns, his eyes as though painted on his face, his nose a bulge, his mouth a line.

His face is real, but the mask draws us. At first we think of the actor behind it. It must be difficult to see, to breathe; perhaps this is why he moves so slowly — he cannot find his way about the stage. But, just as in the doll theater it is said that the faces of those who hold the puppets soon fade, we no longer see them, they no longer disturb us, so — with Noh — the invisible actor becomes truly invisible: we forget him, the face behind the mask is not remembered, the mystery is not disturbed, we believe in it.

And we believe in the mystery precisely because we are *not* shown. The mask is necessary. It is because the second-actor has a face like ours that we do not believe in him. We believe in what we do not recognize. We believe in the mystery.

Noh drama is a rite and a ritual. But whatever its beginnings, whatever its Shinto derivations, whatever Buddhist associations it may incorporate, it is a rite which is no more esoteric than the rite of listening again to a Mozart quartet, or of rereading Proust. It is repetition which gives dignity and no rite may exist without repetition. This is the rite of the Noh-goer. He goes because he has already gone. He owns the texts; he goes — usually — every Sunday; he is an enthusiast, an *aficionado*. There is no other audience for Noh. Not one out of a thousand Japanese has ever seen it. The average Japanese may know its name just as the average American may know Mozart's, but those who have seen the Noh and those who have heard K. 590 are in a like minority. For this audience the performance is indeed a ritual, a bit more so than our Protestant and a bit less than our Catholic. For them the weekly visit to the Noh is like the weekly opera for those who have bought boxes, the weekly concert for those who subscribe to the Philharmonic, except that the pleasure of the Noh enthusiast is more restricted, perhaps more deep. There are no social nor peripheral pleasures, no idea of somehow acquiring that patina called culture. The only pleasure is in a contemplation of the Noh itself.

For this reason the Noh has long been in the hands of "amateurs," unofficial artists who keep it alive. The Gagaku is kept by the Imperial Household, the doll-drama is protected by the state, the Kabuki by one of the largest companies in the amusement industry. Noh is "unofficial" in that a few old families perform, as though for their own amusement and enlightenment, and a few people come to the performances. Everyone except the grand masters has some other job, the week-day job, the job that makes the living. On Sunday they have leisure and can do what they like. Thus Noh is like living-room performances in someone's house; it is like the amateur quartet. It is like this and yet it is unlike it in one respect: the performance is not amateur, it is professional with a rigor which few professional performances know.

No one has ever made a mistake on the Noh stage; no one has ever forgotten a line; there are no stumbling entrances, no halting exits. No indulgence is permitted and when an amateur appears on the stage (and the stage every Sunday contains amateurs who were in the audience the week before) the performance is without error. Just as the archery expert who may sell insurance all week long and visit the master once a week never fails to hit the bull's-eye, so the performances of the Noh are devoid of the in-competence, which has made "amateur" a bad word in our language. Noh is a dilettante theater only if the word is correctly understood. Both performance and attendance are based upon love, respect, and enthusiasm. The ritual of the Noh is like the ritual of the party, the picnic, even the weekly card game. But the party is as formal and meaningful as one in Proust; the picnic is of an elegance that makes one think of Watteau; the card game con-cerns life and death, and devil and angel play together.

The actor in Japanese drama is most important. The Kabuki au-dience goes to see such-and-such with so-and-so *in* it. It is impossi-ble to understand Japanese drama unless one thinks in terms of the prima donna, the star, the premiere ballerina. This is less true of Noh than of Kabuki but it holds — not, indeed, that Noh actors are famous or that the Noh audience goes to see a famous actor in a famous role. Rather, and more generally, it is the actor (any actor) who communicates the experience. Noh is one-person drama, it is like a dramatic monologue, a solo pantomime; it is really all soliloquy. This is seen in the formalization of the drama itself.

At first the stage is empty. Then, from a tiny door, the door of a tea-ceremony room, a door through which one must creep as though humbled or chastised, comes the orchestra, followed by the four- or five-man chorus. They enter hurriedly, unostentatiously, making themselves small, like members of the audience arriving late. From the opposite side of the stage comes the second-actor. He is unobtrusive. He is merely observed as already on the veranda leading to the stage: oh yes, here he comes. There, he is already in place, walking, moving, more or less as you and I walk and move, if more slowly.

But the music is building, the actor on the stage moves to a pillar, as though to get out of the way. For the first time we notice the brocade curtain at the end of the veranda. This is where *he* will appear. The curtain is still, the stage is empty of movement. We wait. Nothing happens. The suspense grows, a suspense which only silence and stillness can build. Then, quite suddenly, the curtain is whipped up; it is jerked from behind. This is a real curtain, not the curtain of the proscenium which insists first that real and make-believe be separate, the proscenium later insisting that they be confused. This is a real, magical curtain which does precisely what a drawn curtain should — it reveals.

There stands the masked first-actor. He appears as though in a kind of transformation. First there is nothing. Then, there he is. He is already supernatural. Slowly, very slowly, he makes his way onto the stage and the play begins. At the second appearance — after the "inner" transformation, and the outer kimono change — the curtain is again whipped up and this time the disclosed monster, angel, ghost, swarms upon the veranda and pounds his way upon the stage, again transformed, again new.

It is the first-actor who dances, who moves, who "sings" — if movement and speech may be called song. And behind this being, behind this mask, stands the actor controlling the Noh, controlling the audience. Because he is masked, because he is both priest and god, he compels an attention that the merely human never commands. We look at him because we cannot look away. Though his movements may irritate us with their slowness, may infuriate because, initially, they seem aimless, arbitrary, yet meticulous, our eyes return again and again, though unwillingly, to his expressionless face, his mask which mirrors all expression.

He holds us. At the same time, we hold him. Were it not for this mutual rapport, Noh would become a charade in pretty clothes. This is what occurs when the Noh is filmed. To a lesser extent is also occurs when opera or Western drama or the Kabuki is filmed. But opera has music, drama has logic, and Kabuki has action. One may enjoy a symphony orchestra without understanding a note of the music — there is so much to look at. But one will not enjoy a live performance of the Bach 'cello suites unless one enjoys Bach. And, even here, there is the music as intermediary between performer and audience. In the Noh there is nothing. There is an ambiguous story, but the text is fragmentary, arbitrary, ambivalent; the music is a part of the stage decor.

There exists only that extraordinary bond between the mind of the actor and the minds of his audience. There is nothing else. It is pure and naked theater.

Zeami has something to say about this: "Sometimes spectators of the Noh say that the moments of 'no action' are the most enjoyable. This is one of the actor's secret arts. . . . When we examine why such moments . . . are enjoyable, we find that it is due to the underlying spiritual strength of the actor which unremittingly holds the attention. He does not relax when the dancing or singing comes to an end . . . but maintains an unwavering inner strength. This feeling of inner strength will faintly reveal itself and bring enjoyment. . . ." For this reason filmed performances are uninteresting. What was moving becomes quaint, what was enlightening evaporates completely. One does not see a movie as one sees the Noh, and the actor does not perform for a camera as he does for a living audience.

The West has nothing like it unless it be the boxing match where the two fighters exist as naturally as fish in a human sea of roarings, spotlights, shouts and exclamations, held and sustained by the sea of humanity of which they are a part, suspended by the thousands of eyes that have made their focal point these two fighting bodies. Between rounds the boxer is dazed, not only because of blows absorbed, but because he has suddenly awakened, because the bond has been snapped, the circuit opened for a minute after three minutes of electrical flow. Two boxers boxing together in a closed room alone would not be boxing, they would not even be able to fight.

Likewise, there is no such thing as a Noh rehearsal. There are placing rehearsals for young actors, there are lines to be learned, but there is no performance unless it takes place amid an audience. This bond is the most important fact of Noh and it is toward this that text, music, decor, costume, all work. Not that all are necessary. Noh works in the proscenium theatre. The context is missing but the most important element is there. Just as the Bach violin partitas could conceivably be performed by someone very clever with a comb and a piece of tissue paper, so the essence of Noh remains, that essence which stops time, makes performer and audience one, which sometimes welds together priest and congregation, which unites the lynching mob. It is this which the actors must first introduce — with the help of the mask, with the entire context of Noh as drama — and then maintain.

Before the actor goes on, he waits in the room on the other side of the brocade curtain. His mask is placed over his face, his costume is arranged, and then he sits before a large full-length mirror, looking at himself. He is preparing. Is he losing himself in the character he imagines? — or is he observing the effect he makes, the better to step outside himself and present it? Both are possible — they are the only possible alternatives. Either he becomes the spirit or else he sees the spirit in his outer form and seeks to present it most effectively. He becomes, or he controls; he loses himself completely, or else so completely controls himself that presentation is possible.

The term "noh" could mean "accomplishment" or "skill" or "talent," and it derives from a verb meaning "to be able" or "to have power." Zeami spoke of the Noh as meaning "elegant imitation" and the music and singing was to "open the ear of the mind" while the dancing was to "open the eyes" of the emotions. "First of all, be a perfect image of the being you are imper-

sonating, then you will also become like him in action," wrote
Zeami and "perfect" is the most important word here. He speaks
of the skin, flesh, and bone of a performance and condemns the actor content with skin alone. When a Noh performance is perfect,
it captivates by impressing with a sense of strength coming from
the bones, a sense of security from the flesh, and a sense of beauty
from the skin. Acting then is "a psychic force which is capable of
excellence resulting from a lifelong effort of training and a careful
choosing of right from wrong." And, above all, when imitating,
"it is important to adjust the act of imitation according to the
nature of the thing," which means that the actor must know
what the thing is.

If an actor tries to show an old man merely by bending his
knees and back he is creating an ugly figure, lacking in strength
and beauty. The old man is required to flower, and by 'flower"
Zeami means that something which arouses and captures the interest. This is accomplished by the actor's responding correctly to
the state of his audience. If they are anticipating they should be
"lightly entertained," but if wandering they should be "startled
into receptivity." They must be taken by surprise. One must
"bewitch the audience." The actor must maintain that state of
balance between himself and the audience, whether he portrays an
old man, a woman, or a warrior; and this state is described as being like "a flower blooming on an old tree."

This bond between actors and audience is a bout. The actor
returns, after the play is over, exhausted; exhausted in the way a
dancer is never exhausted. He has been a god, or else has stood
beside and controlled a god. Whichever, he must rest, he must lie
down, he must sleep. Like the boxer, he had his first bout with

the mirror and, like the boxer, he returns battered, having endured not merely the blows but the consciousness of other wills beating against and finally with his own.

The text is forgotten, the costumes folded, the stage empty, but to those who have seen Noh, to look upon even the empty stage is to remember that naked will, disguised as a god, standing there, demanding and receiving. The experience is religious and, like all religious experiences, it is also aesthetic. Like any sacrificial act, like boxing, like the high mass, it is also cleansing. Though tragedy has not stalked the stage, the effect is catharsis. By becoming one with something not oneself, one is cleansed, made new, and — if only for the moment — made whole.

—1966

The Kyogen

NOH IS USUALLY about gods and spirits, it is idealistic drama which peers deeply into the mysteries of the spirit; Kyogen is always about human beings and even its gods are obviously mortal. It has no use for that ideal face, the mask; it does not need music because there is no mystery to suggest; nor is it slow, stately, or poetic: its language is vernacular and its tempo is faster than life. Kyogen is satyr-play, anti-masque; it is Pyramus and Thisbe to the Noh's Theseus and Hippolyta. Taking place in the kitchen, near the warm hearth, leaving the cold if stately hall to the deities, it is resolutely and resoundly human.

It was human frailty which created Kyogen since it was originally intended to obviate the sublime and unavoidable boredom of the Noh. Though its ancestory is plebeian, though that of the Noh is aristocratic, an alliance was arranged between the two houses and the marriage still holds. Even now a Kyogen is usually sandwiched between two Noh plays, or even between halves of a single drama; even now the marriage shows what all successful marriages must—a dazzling contrast.

The Noh concludes, the last wraith slides away; the Kyogen begins: suddenly the carpenters appear. They open their mouths and we fall from the clouds and land with a bump, just as does one of the gods in their plays. Moved by the Noh, transfigured, a better and ideal world opening before us, our eyes wet with its beauty, we—the audience—become a part of the great and single comic plot when, bounced back into reality by the Kyogen, we discover that we too have two hands and a nose like everyone else, and that those funny people in front of us are ourselves. And we are hilarious because one of the astonishing things about Kyogen is that it is so very funny—not to read, perhaps, but then the text of a Labiche farce or a Keaton film, or even a Molière play, is not that funny to read. Comedy, unlike tragedy, lies in the doing.

The Kyogen doings are based on a slender repertoire of situations. A lord has a stupid servant (always called Taro Kaja, just as Charlot is always Charlot, Buster is always Buster) who cannot tell a fan from an umbrella, or who inadvertently gives away to his mistress his master's philanderings, or who drinks up all the sake and fills up the bottles with hot water and then tries to talk the master into thinking he is getting drunk. Taro is joined by a large cast of comic characters, each as distinctive as himself, just as sublimely stupid, as gloriously sly, as eternally innocent. For it is our foibles which Kyogen celebrates, just as the Noh illuminates our aspirations. Comic situations are as limited as tragic and it is their scarcity which links the great and presumably opposed houses of tears and laughter, which enables great minds to flap the plots over like flapjacks and which shows us that Hamlet and Don Quixote are really first cousins. The audience, after all, has only two minds of which to be and the Kyogen says: Come on, be yourselves.

Not then, for the Kyogen actor the brocades of Noh, those great, living landscapes for the back. Instead, he wears domestic colors—brown, grey, all in checks and squares and diamonds. Clean, neat, starched and common, he is nonetheless ready to run and fall down. And when he races off at the end of the play, it is not, one feels, to that mirrored room of the Noh actor, chamber for meditation, for communion with the mysterious self. No, it is straight for the kitchen and the warm fire and a cup of hot sake taken with smacking lips.

He is a real professional, the Kyogen actor. He delivers fast, is always on his feet, a true stand-up comic. He bubbles over, he aspirates, he is very funny. Yet—and here he shares with the greatest of comedians—he is never vulgar. Zeami, the man who invented Japanese dramaturgy, speaks loud and clear from the depths of the fourteenth century when he says that Kyogen should "kindle the mind to laughter," but that "neither in speech nor in gesture should there be anything low. The jokes and repartee . . . . however funny they may be, should not introduce the vulgar."

Hence, perhaps, the warmth, the charm. In Kyogen one senses that the actor, knowing perfectly well that he is impersonating a comic, also feels that both breeding and goodwill insist that he hide this fact. He is never a wise-guy. He is observing what Zeami himself was probably only observing when he laid down the law that there should be "a tinge of unreality in reality," a "refinement and concentration of all conflicting qualities into one dominant note." This note seems to sound in the ears of only the greatest of comedians: you, a human, must impersonate a human.

And the Kyogen is (if you can put it this way) sublimely human. It celebrates foibles in the way that melodrama celebrates goodness, and that tragedy celebrates devotion. Mistakes, error, sloth, and all of the appetites—these are the stuff of which Kyogen is made. The mirror that it holds up is not the mirror of Noh, the self alone, communing, but a minutely detailed picture of the world as it is, crowded and crawling, like a street-scene seen through the wrong end of a telescope, a world we know quite well but now find rendered hilariously understandable.

It is half the world, and it knows it. It is one pole of human aspiration, just as Noh is the other. The resulting stress, even strain, is what makes the combination so supremely right. The way we would want to be, the way of aspiration, this is Noh. The way we are, the way to acceptance, this is Kyogen. And both roads lead to wisdom.

The Kyogen actor with his air of faint amusement, his just-you-wait-and-see mien, the savoring pucker of a loving artist controlling his comic role—this is a look which says: I know that I am human, only human, with all of our foibles, but this I can accept, just as I can accept the change of seasons, the coming of wrinkles, grey hair and an aching back. This is how things are—my world of Kyogen is your world as well.

—1969

Japan's Avantgarde Theater

ANY AVANTGARDE art is predicated upon its newness and its novelty. When these qualities become sufficiently absorbed the art ceases to be avantgarde and becomes establishment. This is the pattern in all countries and Japan is consequently no exception. In fact, Japan — particularly in its drama — offers a clearer view of this phenomenon than many other countries.

In the late nineteenth century, for example, Shimpa, that naturalistic theatrical form created in direct opposition to the stylization of the Kabuki, was avantgarde. Likewise the Shingeki, which in the early twentieth century was created in opposition to the by then codified and generally accepted Shimpa.

After World War II, Shingeki itself had ceased being a realistic theater — which is to say that realism had turned into mere technique and had become an accepted and unexceptional theatrical mode. Again a new drama rose in opposition to it and it is this which we now still call the avantgarde theater of Japan.

Or, theaters — since one of the attributes of the avantgarde is that it has not yet settled into a single mode which goes by a single name. There is thus as yet no generic term — Kabuki, Shimpa, Shingeki — for these various theaters. They do, however, share both aims and results.

In describing these, perhaps it is best to look at the chronology and to try to indicate where the various common elements among these theaters came from.

First to be noticed is the Japaneseness of the Japanese avant-garde theaters. This is in direct opposition to early Shingeki — which was thoroughly Western in inspiration — and is consequently closer to the Shimpa, one of the aims of which was to be Japanese within a naturalistic setting. The postwar avantgarde from the first insisted upon its peculiar Japaneseness.

(In this it is quite different from other forms of modern Japanese drama. The plays of Kobo Abe or Minoru Betsuyaku, to name but two well-established modern playwrights, are about Japan but the mode is that of the experimental theater of the West. This is as true of Abe's *Friends* as it is of his more avantgarde-seeming happenings and "image theaters." Neither Abe nor Betsuyaku are considered avantgarde. Rather, they are considered variants of Shingeki.)

To identify this Japaneseness one should examine the "look" of the avantgarde theaters. They share much in common and this appearance may be traced back, I think, to a single source. This is the graphic work of Tadanori Yoko-o, a body of illustration which had an enormous influence upon the avantgarde theaters in Japan. The "look" of a Terayama or a Kara production even now reflects Yoko-o's influence.

One of the ploys of any avantgarde manifestation is to take the resolutely unfashionable and make it fashionable. Yoko-o's early work used an iconography which was startling in the "bad taste" involved. He deliberately used an idiom which "art" had not heretofore used.

Specifically, the inspiration was late-Meiji, Taisho, and early-Showa period popular art — that is, the mass art of, roughly, 1910 to 1930. Bright, innocent colors, hard-line cartoon-like drawings; compositions reminiscent of old theatrical bills, menus, newspapers of the period; much use of old photographs, particularly children; abundant picturizations of extreme emotions rendered purposely naïve — tears, laughter; much use of the commercial artifact such as the Victor dog; a general childlike but actually quite sophisticated picture of better, or at least more innocent days. The style was, at the same time, the Japanese version of American pop-art (which made its instant acceptance the more understandable) but it lacked both the irony and the cynicism of an Andy Warhol. Rather, it consisted of a new, usable, and — to the postwar generation — completely novel vocabulary.

Yoko-o's style was rapidly accepted. All of his iconography had been, if not despised, ignored. It was hence invisible until Yoko-o reinvented it. It had been found banal and embarrassing; now it was found (true to the principles involved) avantgarde. Yoko-o created a minor revolution in graphics and even now, nearly twenty years later, and after the artist himself has gone onto other styles, one sees its remains.

This is particularly true in the avantgarde theaters. We are also, in discussing this style, involved in describing a *zeitgeist,* since manifestations appeared on a number of fronts almost simultaneously. There remains a large question at to who influenced whom — whether one may describe Yoko-o as the founder or whether he was in turn influenced by one of the dramatists. The case is a bit like the beginnings of cubism in France: it occurred simultaneously in many places, yet a non-painter, Apollinaire, is often given credit for formulating the style.

Certainly Yoko-o enjoyed a mutual influence with the first major avantgarde figure in postwar Japan. This was Tatsumi Hijikata, the modern dancer, whose theater — the Asubesutokan — many be regarded as the cradle of the contemporary avantgarde dance movement. During the fifties and into the sixties, Hijikata presented a series of dramatic presentations which were unlike anything Japan had seen. Though nominally dance, they were at the same time silent plays, and they were distinguished by their length, their apparent irrationality, their intended boredom, and their surprising juxtapositions.

It was, and remains, a theater of poverty: dancers are in rags, or in strange combinations of Japanese dress. Finery from the Taisho period — large picture hats, for example — were used, as were Meiji-style bat-wing umbrellas. Hijikata's picture was not only the end of the world but, especially, the end of Japan. The stage resembled a flea-market and the effect was, purposely, poignant. Here is the postwar wasteland, filled with spastic cripples holding aloft these pathetic emblems of a vanished civilization.

What was held aloft, however, were not the art objects of Japan but, specifically, those objects which once had a use, which were once a part of popular culture. The theatrical influence on Hijikata, to the extent that there was one, was the side-show, the *yose* theater, the vaudeville review — the mundane and common and vulgar entertainments of prewar Japan. This world is still on view, since it is still a part of the avantgarde and one sees it in Hijikata's works, as well as those of his pupil, Yoko Ashikawa, and those who broke away from him.

Dance and drama originally almost identical in the postwar Japanese avantgarde later separated — the former become a dance-theater known as Buto, a neologism coined in contrast to Budo, classical Japanese dance. Though Hijikata was the best known exponent of this form, his teacher, Kazuo Ono (himself influenced by the expressionist dance of Mary Wigman and Harold Kreutzberg) had other pupils as well, such as Akira Kasai.

The pupils of Ono (as well as those of Kasai and Hijikata, in-cluding the many former students who broke away from their teachers), later formed their own Buto troupes and there are now a great many of them including the Dairakudakan Group, the all-male Sebi Troupe, the all-female Ariadone, and a large number of solo dancers the most best-known of which is probably Min Tanaka.

The contemporary Buto style retains the basic Ono-Hijikata vocabulary but its scenic representation has now refined itself into a kind of primitivism (body paint, nudity, rope, twine, wood, etc.) in which a new shamanism seems often the theme. The Taisho-look as seen in the earliest Buto performances, and as ex-emplified by the Yoko-o stage designs has now disappeared from this form.

Yoko-o knew Hijikata and his work and also designed posters for him in his early days. In the matter of style and iconography I would imagine, however, that these two artists influenced each other. Among those writers and directors who came later, however, I think that the influence of Yoko-o is paramount.

Certainly there is no doubt about this influence on Terayama Shuji, whose Tenjo Sajiki Theater during the early Sixties became the single most important avantgarde group. Terayama himself, also known as one of Japan's best modern poets, created in his plays a world which shares something with that of Hijikata (for whom he also wrote) and which took over the iconography of Yoko-o (who did all of his early posters and some of his early stage designs) complete.

His world is the ruined but still genteel era of Taisho and early Showa. The Victor dog is there, and advertisements for prewar cigarettes; the Japanese traveling circus is in evidence; pathetic efforts at Western finery, feather boas, ormolu-framed mirrors; and equally pathetic remnants from a Japanese past: country-striped kimono, Meiji-period overcoats, Sherlock-Holmes hats, etc.

These illustrate an invariable theme: a boy is menaced by an older woman, often his mother. He is saved, if he is to be saved, by a girl his own age or slightly older — who often sexually initiates him. He is also sometimes befriended by an older man but one whose sexuality remains indeterminate. This is the "story" of both the early *Kegawa no mari* (Mink Marie), and most of his later adaptations (Bartok's *Miraculous Mandarin*) and some of his films.

The story is obviously and purposely melodrama. Whatever personal significance it had to Terayama (and it must have considerable to appear so regularly), we are not invited to take it seriously. We are invited to see through it. Just as Yoko-o invites us to view this iconography from a distance, so Terayama asks us to see his theater dispassionately. Just as the artist purposely uses popular clichés in his designs, so the dramatist purposely uses the crudest excesses of prewar popular melodrama. The result has ironic intentions, is deliberately child-like, is often purposely comic and suggests a kind of genial anarchy.

Anarchy, genial or otherwise, is often the expressed aim of Japanese avantgarde theater. The most extreme is the Zero Jikken Group of Yoshihiro Kato. This troupe of young men and women gives only occasional and usually spontaneous performances, often involving complete nudity — a rarity in Japan — and mostly consisting of orgiastic dances and an amount of implied sado-masochism. Here something of a "primitive" Japan is perhaps suggested, but at the same time (as in their use of combinations of Western and Japanese dress) the days of early Showa are also there, as is also the "wasteland" implication common to all of these theaters.

Frankly anarchial — and for a time the most important of the avantgarde theaters in Japan — is the Jokyo (Situation) Gekijo of Juro Kara. Here the influence is popular early Showa melodrama, the *yose* variety theater, comic books, old trashy movies, country Kabuki — all molded into a often powerful theatrical experience. We are still in the wasteland and the Yoko-o look is still in evidence (the artist did posters for the Jokyo Gekijo as well) but the sometimes autobiographical preoccupations of Terayama are missing. Kara's preoccupations, though often hidden behind a façade of playful dialogue and outrageous stage effects, are usually at least covertly political.

His is the single one of the avantgarde theaters which is satirical and his targets are a part of contemporary Japan. From his earliest play, the prodigal *Long John Silver,* through such successes as *Shojo Kamen,* Kara has consistently criticized postwar Japan, particularly the ruling classes. He had indeed become a spokesman for the dissident.

This was acknowledged a number of years ago when the police got after him and several of his productions were banned. Such is Japanese law that he evaded this by holding the performances in a large red tent pitched at locations only announced just before the play was to begin. And such was his following that young people all over Tokyo found out the location and attended the event. He rarely returned to a theater and his plays were still held in the red tent at the most unlikely places and the underground still found out where these were and every seat (or most often cushion) was taken. If not only the avantgarde, but all Japanese theater had one vital, living drama it was the Jokyo Gekijo.

If it is the nature of the avantgarde to scandalize society, it is the nature of society to "civilize" the avantgarde. Mainly this is accomplished, in Japan as elsewhere, through commercialization. When a large department-store combine discovered that the avantgarde sold and that a number of the young would buy, one of the results was a Juro Kara spectacle called *The Shitaya-Mannen-cho Story,* a kind of latter-day *Dreigroschenoper* set in downtown Tokyo. Here criticism turned to fun and dissidence to entertainment. The entire expensive production was very slickly directed (not by Kara) and was a sell-out success. It was also the end of Kara as an avantgarde dramatist.

Kara himself shows the influence of Hijikata and was originally with Yoshiyuki Fukuda (since gone into commercial theater) and his Seigei Troupe. Another affiliate of Fukuda, and friend of Kara, was Makoto Sato, who showed the Yoko-o look in its most elegant form in productions such as *Sada Abe's Dog* and — one of the most perfect of Japan's postwar productions — the Brecht-Weill *Mahagonny Singspiele.*

There is indeed something of a parallel between the avantgarde of the Weimar Republic and that of postwar Japan. Both are not "serious" in the manner of the theaters which proceeded them, both are full of "prewar" materials, and in both you are intended to "see through" the ostensible and glimpse an attitude which is at once critical and/or ironic. Finally, there is a strong nationalist unity — the "Germanness" of Brecht and Toller, the "Japaneseness" of Kara and Terayama. This attitude is often a put-on, its intentions are commonly satirical, but the fact that it is there indicates some kind of search for an identity, even a national one, in a world which is fragmented.

This search is often the theme of one of the most talented of the avantgarde directors, Tadashi Suzuki, who was originally with the Waseda Sho-gekijo and is now, mainly, independent. His extremely successful *Trojan Women,* based loosely on the Euripides, is an example. Within the framework of the whole lost Trojan War, he reconstructs a parallel drama in which all the Japanese theatrical styles are suggested in their chronological order — from early Sarugaku right up to the Shimpa. At the same time the costumes and properties change during the course of drama and we end up in the tawdry glitter of postwar Japan. As the women of Troy search for some kind of meaning in the ruins, Suzuki presents a cavalcade — often highly ironic — of a similar Japanese search.

The same is true of Suzuki's later productions, particularly his dramatization of another Euripides tragedy, *The Bacchae,* the structure of which was that it could be performed in various languages simultaneously (as it was — English-Japanese) with the Milwaukee Theater. Here the resulting babel reflected the search for unity that is the theme of the play. His *House of Atreus* (a collage from the Greek tragedians) is about a unity lost and its style is correspondingly diverse — Greek tunics, Noh robes, Meiji overcoats. The stage is filed with vain searching. Orestes and Elektra stand under a small cloud which rains only on them.

The search is everything. It is both moving and meaningful. When the goal is achieved the Japanese avantgarde theaters at once lose their immediacy — and their standing as avantgarde. An example is Yutaka Higashi and his Tokyo Kid Brothers Group, a breakaway section of Terayama's Tenjo Sajiki. Higashi's *Golden Bat* started off as dissident theater and, as such, was seen abroad. When he embraced the international brotherhood of hippyism and the easy solution, however, his productions lost their Japanese immediacy as well as their integrity. Something of the same kind happened to Tetsu Yamazaki and his Tsumbo Sajiki, a breakoff group from Kara and the Jokyo Gekijo. Here the director found an answer to his problems in the old-fashioned style of the *chambara* or sword-fight plays. But his productions turned into pastiche, and then into pure nonsense. Though still interesting and representing nothing approaching the sell-out of Higashi's, Yamazaki's offerings now too often resemble the light-hearted and meaningless entertainment he was originally parodying to lend some insight into the disordered and chaotic postwar world.

These theaters share a number of similarities. All are almost excessively concerned with the past (in itself, to be sure, a Japanese preoccupation), yet all see this past not in Japan's long history but in that small segment known to the fathers of the directors but not to the directors themselves — since all, except Hijikata, grew up during or after the war.

All see this period (late Taisho, early Showa) as either an idyllic age of innocence or as a kind of junk yard from which bits and pieces may be scavenged to decorate an otherwise featureless postwar world. At the same time there is a definite aversion to "art" as such and, indeed, being anti-art is one of the stances of the Japanese avantgarde. (This is carried to extremely interesting extremes in the work of Kohei Tsuka, who has shown the fragility and sometimes pathetic pretensions of popular theater in works such as his *Sutorippa Monogatari* (The Story of a Stripper). Finally, there is a purposeful frivolity (even, or particularly, in the work of Kara) which seeks serious solutions in laughter, an earnest use of the *fausse-naïf* (the Yoko-o look), and, consequently — except in the work of Kara and Hijikata — a kind of sentimentality, upside down though it is.

These avantgarde theaters are purposely slight: they are intended to be. Consequently they lend themselves all too readily to commercial exploitation. No one was surprised when Terayama, by then already half-establishment, used a name commercial designer for his costumes. No one is alarmed at the commercialism of Yutaka Higashi. At the same time there are signs that these avantgarde theaters are evolving into something further.

One of the more recent groups is that called the Tenkei Gekijo, where the often wordless plays of Shogo Ota are performed. In *Water Station* a water faucet slowly drops. During the next two hours, slowly, very slowly, tattered folk with bundles and piled baby-carriages cross the stage, pausing at the dripping faucet.

We are recognizably in the wasteland of postwar Japanese theater, but it has now been rarified into a single prop (the faucet) and a single action (stopping for water). This minimal theater, slow as a Noh play and almost as spare, is theater reduced to its essentials.

The wordplay and topical political references of Juro Kara have been pushed even further by the machinegun-like delivery of Hideki Noda and his Yume-no-Yuminsha group, a troupe which has now been accorded something of the popularity of the Jokyo Gekijo. In addition, the new dramatist-director, Eriko Watanabe has been called the "Female Kara," and the same line is being followed by another woman, Koharu Kisaragi, both of whom specialize in the amusing outrage which is one of the attributes of the Japanese theatrical avantgarde.

An indication of further developments is Yoshio Oida and his Yoshi et Cie. This Shingeki actor has been working completely independently of the Japanese avantgarde: he has in fact not even been working in Japan, he has been mainly with Peter Brook in Europe. Yet in his way he shares many of the same assumptions. Fully grounded in traditional Japanese dramatic forms — the Noh, the Kyogen, the *gidayu* and *joruri* of Bunraku and Kabuki — in addition to having been a very successful Shingeki actor, he has created a theater which quite seriously seeks its roots in the past and at the same time displays a concern for the present which is neither frivolous nor cynical.

His best work, the collection of "ritual games" called *Ame-Tsuchi,* has never been seen in Japan, though it has been widely viewed in Europe and America. Here he uses the *Kojiki,* Japan's most ancient record to create a theatrical experience which aims at isolating, precisely, the Japaneseness of the elements he has put together. (No one in Japan's avantgarde theater is, in this sense, more "Japanese" than Oida.) The medium through which it is shown, however, is completely separate — it is the rituals and bouts of that most Japanese of sports, *kendo.* This creates a double parallel — aided but not explained by the language, which is archaic Japanese and no more understandable to a Japanese audience than, say, middle-English would be to a British or American audience. There is no evidence of any Yoko-o influence but it, like other Yoko-o influenced works, is plainly collage-theater. Oida's concern, however, is the opposite of that of many of Japan's avantgarde directors. He is not trying to show the seams, and not attempting to indicate the many ill-fitting parts of Japanese life. Rather (and in this sense he is close to Hijikata) he is attempting to present a whole. Here he is close to the Buto troupes in Japan whose work he has not in all probability seen and who have in turn never seen any of Oida's work. Both Buto and Oida are very much of the earth. As in all Japanese dance, the dancers are not only heavily placed, pelvis low, feet flat, they also seem to derive their vitality from the earth: in Oida the gliding of the Noh-like steps, the sudden Judo-like leaps and returns, in Buto the dancers themselves who, clay-colored, grope upward, as though toward light. It might seem strange to compare Oida's elegant and inventive constructions with the simplistic and repetitive structures of Buto yet they have much in common. Both are striving for a unity, in the very face of an avantgarde which is attempting to display only disparity and incongruity.

In works such as these one sees indications of a further avantgarde, a theatrical form which is new, original and novel, and one which creates a new iconography, a new set of images, and a new reflection of the times.

It is the nature of the avantgarde to move rapidly into new, and often opposite, forms. Now that the Yoko-o look has taken over even TV advertising, now that Terayama is given official recognition, now that even Kara has his own commercial sponsors, now that all of this is occurring, one may expect a new avantgarde and there are signs that it is already beginning.

—1979

The Strata of Japanese Drama

JAPAN, UNLIKE most other countries, retains most of its earlier dramatic forms. The Noh, the Kyogen, Bunraku and Kabuki, stretching from the 16th century on, are still regularly performed, each in its individual type of theater. Bugaku, a ninth-century dance-drama and Shimpa, a late 19th-century type of melodrama, are still to be seen. In the larger cities of Japan one may, in one week, see almost all the forms which drama has taken, all in their original states, a series of theatrical structures, each quite separate—dramatic strata comparable to the layers of a giant geological specimen, a ringed cross-section of the tree of Japanese drama.

Each stratum petrifies, retaining its own characteristics, frozen apparently forever yet still alive since each style is studied, performed, and retains its audience. It is as though one went to Rome and found there theaters specializing in Plautus done in Latin in the original style, playhouses where the *commedia dell' arte* was retained in its perfection, and halls where Pirandello is performed in the manner of 1925.

One may also watch this dramatic solidification at work. Since World War II, Shingeki—the most recent of Japanese theatrical forms—has slowly petrified, a process quite visible and one which ensures the longevity which so distinguishes the Japanese drama as a whole.

Just as Shimpa (with real actresses and contemporary plots) originally saw itself as a rebellion against the rigidities of the Kabuki, so the new Shingeki (literally, new theater) saw itself in rebellion against what it called the artificialities of all prior

Japanese drama. Beginning early in this century, spurred by the example of the modern Western stage, Shingeki wanted to create a free, vital, meaningful and above all contemporary drama, directly relevant, realistic—even naturalistic—in style.

Now, not 75 years after its inception, the Shingeki has become as stylized, as mannered if you will, as the Shimpa it hoped to supplant. Though new plays continue to be written for the Shingeki they in turn are influenced by the form which the theater has taken. Shingeki actors are taught a special naturalistic way of speaking but since this is not, by its nature, natural, this too becomes a convention. The playwrights, admiring and emulating the well-tailored Western play of the mid-20th century, now create inside a system of unities as rigid as, if different from, those of the Noh.

In recent years one has seen the same phenomenon occur in the dramatic form which succeeded the Shingeki—variously named avantgarde theater, underground theater—the drama of which Shuji Terayama, Juro Kara, Makoto Sato and Tadashi Suzuki are the leading playwrights and directors.

Originally, in the 1960s, Japanese avantgarde drama was in full rebellion against the rigidity and unnaturalness of the Shingeki. The new theater was supposed to be spontaneous, free, and above all personal. At the same time, it was supposed to be political; society was to be criticized, indicted if possible, and freedom of the individual was to be respected and even celebrated.

Now, not 20 years later, the drama of Juro Kara, though still performed in the *al fresco* surroundings of his famous tent, is as rigid in its way as the Bunraku, and its very structure has become predetermined. The plays of Makoto Sato have become doctrinaire political melodramas. And the iconography of Shuji Terayama, originally so startling, became as expected as that of the Kabuki.

One may observe this petrification in other countries, to be sure—look at the fustian standards of most modern Shakespearian productions. One cannot, however, see the entire dramatic history of a country at a glance as it were. And usually, in other countries, the achievements of one epic are buried under the experiments of the next. In Japan, in contradistinction, one sees everything, from the beginnings to this temporary end.

There are various ways of accounting for it. One certainly is the enormous prestige given the artist, the creator. Every word becomes law, every mannerism an iron model for later generations. The spoken word tends to become the written word in very short order in Japan: the collected works of Terayama (unthinkable 20 years ago) are already gathered on the shelf.

Perhaps the most important reason behind this urge to mannerist drama, behind this mighty slab of visible theatrical history, however, is a Japanese mode of thought, a way of thinking which is seen in all aspects of Japanese civilization and so thoroughly imbues that culture. Its drama may be seen as a paradigm of the whole.

We have no name for this manner of thought, though we are certainly familiar with it ourselves—at the most, if we have a word it is pejorative: stereotyped thinking, clichéd thought, etc. The same process in Japan is considered much more respectable and is, indeed, vital. Its qualities are found in the noun *kata* which the dictionary defines as a model, a mold, a matrix, or a pattern, a cut, a form.

Anything at all, an action, a word, a thought, is soon broken down into its basic elements. The result, the kata as it were, is then taken as emblematic of the thing it represents. In other words, reality is once removed, the signifier becomes the signified; manner becomes mannerism and reality becomes gesture.

This results in instant style. In the theater, as we have seen, the style becomes the drama itself, content becomes form. Such forms are self-sufficient; perfected, they last forever. It is for this reason, among others, that the strata of Japanese drama remain.

Much can be said in defense of the kata and its products. Though it makes spontaneous, realistic, democratic drama (and thinking) impossible, it also provides that necessary step away from reality which is the prerequisite of all art, and it imposes those limitations without which true artistic freedom is impossible. Also, and almost incidentally, it allows us to see—in Japan alone—the entire and mighty vista of a national drama, a whole stratum of theatrical history.

—1981

V

Women in Japanese Cinema

ONE DAY, a number of years ago, I was speaking with director Shiro Toyoda. We were talking about film-acting and I asked why the men were usually such poor actors and why the women were almost invariably so good. He said that it was only natural: the Japanese woman from childhood is forced to play a role — more so than in most countries. She is her father's daughter, then her husband's wife, then her son's mother. From the earliest age she learns to mask her true feelings and to counterfeit those she does not feel. One of the results is that the Japanese woman becomes a consummate actress. "You could take almost anyone, put her up on the screen, and she would do very well," said Toyoda.

This seems small compensation for such a restricted life. Acting it is, but it is also dissimulation and — eventually — bad faith. Born into a position still openly regarded as inferior, given the most limited choices, Japanese women are expected to shuttle between kitchen and bed, to be cheerful with the fretful male, to manage the household economies, to deny herself as a person and yet, somehow, find fulfillment within her narrow confines.

Okusan, the Japanese word for wife, literally means "the one inside." By extension it means the one who cannot get out. The male criticism most often leveled against Japanese women, and one before which all but the bravest would cringe, is *onna rashiku nai* which means "unwomanly." It is usually heard when a woman has done anything to realize herself in human rather than "feminine" terms.

The dilemma of the Japanese woman is acute. She cannot even

seek solace in the tokenism to which men in the West are now resorting. Legally, women can remain nearly as helpless and dependent as children — wards of their fathers and husbands. Economically, if they try to make a career, the double standard continues and they are often paid less than a man in the same position. Socially, if they remain single, or work for a living, or get divorced, they are subject to varying degrees of opprobrium. In old age, a kind of freedom is attained only because a woman has by then become useless.

In no other country as advanced as Japan is woman still so frankly regarded as chattel. The double standard is so ingrained that it is almost taken for granted; consequently, no attempts are made to conceal it. The manipulation of women for economic, social, and sexual purposes is openly displayed, and its rightness is seldom questioned. One would not, indeed, expect men to doubt a system so beneficial to themselves. But in Japan, more often than not, the women also seem to subscribe to the rightness of their own oppression. They submit and endure; or they enter professions designed to entertain men where, unless vigilant, they become as predatory as the males they serve. Sincerely, cynically, or hopelessly they collaborate.

There is one quarter of this vexed area, however, that differs markedly from similar states in the West: Japanese women and their limited province have been meticulously and honestly observed. To a limited extent this has occurred in Japanese literature and drama. Overwhelmingly, it has occurred in the cinema. An extraordinary dossier has been built up of films devoted to women and their various problems. That this should have occurred in a society so frankly male chauvinist is surprising: films, after all, are made by men and financed by them.

One of the reasons is that until recently a predominantly female cinema audience was actively promoted. Going to the movies is traditionally one of the freedoms allowed a woman, since it is presumed that she has both the time and inclination to do so. Yet, if one compares Japanese women in film with those of the West, one sees little of the hopefully compensating glamour and elegance cynically given Norma Shearer or Lana Turner, almost nothing of the harmless independence allowed Brigitte Bardot or Audrey Hepburn and their more recent counterparts, and nothing at all of the mock-dangerous bitch freedom granted Bette Davis or Joan Crawford.

The main reasons for the reliability of Japan's films about women is that, as a whole, Japanese cinema has until recently concerned itself with a faithful delineation of *all* aspects of Japanese life. It did not become a dream factory until much later than most national cinemas. There is consequently a truthfulness in the presentation of women that is largely missing from films in the West.

And there is another consideration. Any serious film director is concerned not only with meticulous representation but also with a kind of drama which must, by its nature, question the ethical rightness of things as they are. There are obviously great exceptions — in Japan that of Yasujiro Ozu at once suggests itself. Usually, however, a director is drawn to situations with maximum dramatic potential. Invariably that potential is provided by strife and friction between the individual and his environment. In the Japanese woman, Japanese directors have discovered the perfect protagonist. This does not mean that Japanese directors are feminists — even Kenji Mizoguchi, though he is often so described. It means rather that these directors in seeking objectivity as well as dramatic revelation have, naturally, shown Japanese women as they are.

Of all Japanese directors it was perhaps Mikio Naruse who best understood the position of Japanese women and, consequently, the nature of their dilemma. Certainly, when he wanted to delineate the close confines of life, to show the hopelessness of all attempts at escape, it was women he chose to carry his "message." Other directors have responded similarly. When Keisuke Kinoshita and Kon Ichikawa have criticized existing Japanese social standards it is often women who serve as their protagonists. When Susumu Hani wished to show optimistic hopelessness and when Shohei Imamura wanted to show doomed intransigence, they did so through stories about women. It is through women that Toyoda portrays lost innocence and thwarted bravery. And when Mizoguchi comments pessimistically upon the fruitless journeyings of all humankind, it is through women that the dark nature of life is revealed.

In the performances of the actresses chosen by these great directors there is, moreover, an extraordinary sense of truthfulness and reality. Compared with the dramatic honesty of Setsuko Hara, Hideko Takamine, Sachiko Hidari, the performances of many Western screen actresses seem hardly more than the manipulated posturings that they are. It is perhaps only in the Japanese film that women have been consistently allowed to be themselves. It should be added, however, that it is only in the film that this has been allowed.

The paradox is striking. The single honest cinematic portrait of women has occurred in a country where honesty on the part of women is not tolerated. Not that this has ever been remarked upon in Japan, where openness of such matters all but disarms criticism. What remains is a body of film which reflects with undismayed clarity just what it means to be a woman in Japan. For this, as for all small blessings, one ought to be grateful.

—1976

The Japanese Eroduction

BOTH ECONOMICALLY and psychologically, the eroduction (a Japanese portmanteau-term coined from 'erotic production') is an interesting cinematic phenomenon. In the days of fallen box office receipts it at least made back its costs; in times of empty movie theaters, it played to half-full houses; even now the eroduction continues to command the attention of a loyal if small audience.

One of the reasons for this is that Japan, unlike other civilized countries, has no porno houses. The eroductions are the limpest of soft-core, and though there is much breast and buttock display, though there are simulations of intercourse, none of the working parts are ever shown. Indeed, one pubic hair breaks an unwritten but closely observed code. Though this last problem is solved by shaving the actresses, the larger remains: how to stimulate when the means are missing.

The rigidity of Japanese law in this regard is to be observed in film-showing as a whole. Japanese production must remain within certain limits and when it does not, as was the case with certain Nikkatsu pictures, the company is sued by the Metropolitan Police and a full scale court case follows. Imported films also are no exception to the general rule. Many are rendered chaotic because so many scenes are missing; others are diffcult to follow because the film goes out of focus (an alternative to snipping) during nude scenes; *I Am Curious—Yellow* had forty-one scenes blacked out with the title 'Censored.' A further curiosity was the Japanese presentation of *Woodstock.* In several of the scenes nude couples wander in the distance. Though perhaps unnoticed in many countries, the sharp eyes of the Japanese censor instantly detected this irregularity. A number of employees were equipped with small scraping needles and painstakingly picked the emulsion from the offending parts. When the film was projected the distant strolling couples consequently seemed girded with fireworks. Though this called instant attention to what the censors were presumably attempting to hide, the letter of the law had been observed and this result satisfies all censors everywhere.

In Japan, consequently, the eroduction is needed — small outlet for prurient interest or simple curiosity being found elsewhere. Though any number of illegally imported blue films and tapes are around, they are expensive, difficult to obtain and dangerous to show. For the average, interested moviegoer, the eroduction is all that there is.

Thus, unlike other countries where a free access to pornography has resulted in a satisfied curiosity, a stilled prurience, and emptier and emptier porno houses, Japan retains a compulsive and relatively obsessed audience. There are perhaps deeper psychological reasons for this, as may be apparent later in these notes, and in any event attendance is still good enough that the eroduction business remains a solvent one.

At the height of eroduction production twenty small companies made some two hundred such pictures each year. The shooting-time for each remains short — a week at the most; studios are seldom used, rather actual apartments, houses, etc., are seen; wages are low; and the cost of making such a film can be quite reasonable.

The released film is triple-billed and leased to a distributing chain which owns its own theaters. There were in Tokyo over twenty such chains (Kanto Films, Okura Productions, Tokyo

Kyoe, Roppo, etc.) and the profits from the film are divided in
such a way that from the per-picture average admission price more
than one quarter goes to the original producing company, less
than one quarter to the distribution company, and one half to the
theater.

This division would seem unfair to a production company own-
ing no theaters, but there are actually very few such. Usually, the
production company, the distribution chain, and the theater
management all belong to the same corporation. The profits are
therefore both total and considerable. There were over one hundred eroduction theaters in Tokyo (and probably nearly one thousand in all of Japan) with an average capacity of eight-hundred per
house; they are open daily from ten in the morning to ten at
night, and they are always partially filled. Given the small original
budget and the low cost of overhead, the profits are considerable.

The situation is somewhat analogous to that of the porno
houses in America where the product costs little, upkeep is
negligible, and admission prices are high. Differences would include the amounts of money authorities must sometimes be paid
to allow public showings, and a capricious public which is not to
be depended upon.

In Japan, the eroduction is the only type of picture that retains
an assured patronage. The mass audience has fallen off in the last
decade. Two of the majors (Shintoho and Daiei) are no longer in
existence, Nikkatsu has gotten into trouble trying to turn out
high-class porno, and the movie finances of Toho, Toei, and
Shochiku (as differentiated from their other income sources) cannot be described as good. There exist, however, smaller, isolated

audiences — and among these none is more faithful than the eroduction audience.

An assured audience means a standardized product. It is only in times of economic disaster that different formulas are tried and experimentation is indulged. If commercial cinema in Japan is now changing its content along with its form, it is only because the assured audience has largely disappeared. The eroduction, however, has its own loyal audience and this has resulted in its becoming a codified form of entertainment. Like the spectacle, the musical, the sword-fight *chambara*, the woman's-film — all cinematic forms which enjoyed a stable audience — the eroduction is formula-film

Thus, as a genre, the eroduction is predetermined. Since the audience knows what it is to get, it need not be informed. Consequently, the films' titles are decorative rather than descriptive. *Intercourse Before Marriage* (*Konzen Kosho*); *I Can't Wait for Night* (*Yoru Made Matenai*); *Wriggling* (*Notauchi*) — all these tell nothing about their respective contents; they merely make the ritual statement of intent to titillate, the presumed intention of all eroductions.

Likewise, the length of each film is predetermined. Since each is intended to be shown with two others, the ideal length decided upon is 6,500 feet, or 70 minutes. Further codifications are then introduced into the structure of the film itself. In theory, directors are instructed to aim at some kind of sex scene every five minutes; in practice, however, it has proved almost impossible to construct a story-line which allows this, with the results that sex scenes are sometimes fewer but longer.

Also predetermined, though perhaps not so consciously, is the interior shape of the film. One comes to recognize the component parts, just as in the *jidai-geki* one comes to expect the final sword fight, in the Western, the last shoot out. In the eroduction these necessary parts would be: establishing sequence, plot sequence, defiling sequence, consequence sequence, and concluding sequence. The connecting tissue may vary with the story, but all or some of the predetermined sequences are invariable.

Since the ostensible intent of the eroduction is to arouse, the establishing sequence usually shows the beginning if not the conclusion of a sexual act. Common among these are: tipsy bar hostess being escorted home by inflamed customer; hiking girls being offered and accepting rides from plainly untrustworthy gentlemen in automobiles; unmotivated sexual acts during which conversation establishes that this is her first time. From these beginnings grow scenes which establish that sexual union is taking place.

The plot sequence follows at once. This establishes that: the drunken hostess has really fallen into the hands of a white (or yellow) slaver; the girls are not to be shown the good time they had perhaps expected but, rather, are to be painfully raped by numbers of men; the despoiler of the repentent ex-virgin was not really interested in those now wasted charms — rather, he was really captured by those of a virginal younger sister, etc.

With such tragic complications occurring so soon, one rightly suspects that Japanese eroductions are about something other than the joys of sexual union. The next sequence confirms this — it is about the denigration of women. Bar hostess, goodtime girls, ex-virgin — all are given a very bad time. Common are scenes

where, in order to escape, women must run naked through the
fields or the streets; scenes where nude or near-nude women are
overtaken in muddy rice-paddies, knocked down, mauled, and
dirtied by their attackers; scenes where women are blackmailed into or are in other ways compelled to give themselves to various
perversions, the most overwhelmingly common being: tied up,
hung by wrists, savagely beaten, otherwise mistreated with sticks,
lighted candles, and — odd, but an eroduction favorite — long-
handled shoe-horns.

The consequences of such excess are depicted in the following
sequences. These are various and include women — never men —
coming to see the error of their ways through the humiliations of
venereal disease and unwanted pregnancy. Among the more spectacular, however — and occurring often enough to deserve some
comment — is that though the attackers are shown simulating
every symptom of unbridled lust except the ultimate, it is eventually they who most suffer. Having finally achieved his way, the
hero is suddenly unable to perform. This is not, as one might expect, seen as a consequence of his own rashness; rather, it is
always, somehow, the woman's fault. (Naturally, this failure is
never once seen as human and amusing; indeed, as entertainment,
the eroduction is unique in being both risible and humorless.) The
failure is a tragedy for which woman is to blame.

This leads directly to the concluding sequence where repentance
and remorse are the emotions most often simulated. If the girl has
been bad, she will now be good; if merely unfortunate, she will
now be prudent; if hurt, she must simply live with the knowledge
of an abortion or a ruined younger sister; if dead (as she is in a surprising number of instances) short shrift is made of her personal

existence — rather, she becomes a symbol for the general dangerousness of sex.

If she is dead she has often become so as a result of the impotent sequence. Unable to express baffled emotions, the man resorts to strangling, shooting knifing, etc. (A typical scene occurred in *Black Snow* (*Kuroi Yuki*), a film for which Nikkatsu was early taken to court: the impatient young man unable to express himself in any other way blew out the brains of his girl friend just as she was climaxing in response to his dextral stimulation.) Since, somehow, it was all the woman's fault anyway, the eroduction audience (entirely male, watching a film made entirely by males) finds that this murder is to be regarded sympathetically. It was perhaps unkind, but, after all the hero was experiencing the worst humiliation a man can know, so what else was he to do?

More often, however, man and woman agree to part. After such extended sexual encounters, such pain, such pleasure, the feeling is that it was somehow not worth it. They go their separate ways, sadder, wiser, and the screen darkens. This conclusion is, when you consider it, surprising in a film the announced aim of which was titillation.

But then, like most formula-film, the eroduction is of two minds about its subject. Unable to dwell upon a detailed examination of the sex act as is, say, American pornography, the eroduction must sublimate and take that path which occasionally reaches the summits of art in other kinds of film. All the way along, however, it hankers after what it cannot legally have and its compromises do damage to its already myopic view of reality. American pornography is kept forever on its elemental level because, showing all, it need do nothing else; Japanese eroductions have to do something else since they cannot show all. The stultified impulse has created some extraordinary works of art, a few films among them. None of these, however, are found among eroductions. What the Japanese genre has done is to reflect or create a kind of mythology.

The producers of the eroduction believe that they have discovered a money-making recipe; the patrons of the eroduction think they have found a harmless and inexpensive way of killing a few hours. Both, however, would seem to share further assumptions, and these one must deduce. In main they share a belief, a myth — and the denominator of this common agreement is invariable: to be completely enjoyed, a woman must be completely denigrated.

How different are the various myths suggested by the pornography of other countries. There, even if an amount of sadism is involved, it is always plainly labeled, never suggested as the norm — something which invariably occurs in Japanese eroductions. Though the woman in Western pornography may be a bit more forward than is common in Western life, her only motivation is to have and to give a good time. She is bold, even brazen, but this suits her audience. Indeed, if a man did not require that kind of woman he probably would not be sitting in a porno house.

The Japanese eroduction is very different. Woman must be denigrated and she must deserve to be. The ways in which this is shown are various, but the conclusions are indentical. Often, for example, the woman has had some prior experience. Since she is no longer a virgin, she is ritually unclean and, therefore it would seem, deserves all that she gets. Again, however, if the woman is still a virgin, her culpability is evidenced in other ways. A simple crush or mere attraction for some young, clean-cut type suffices. He shortly vanishes from the film, his sole function having been to uncover her low, animal nature. Or a man may not even be involved. Instead, she is observed in amorous dalliance with another girl — a spectacle some men find exciting — which establishes her worthlessness at once.

One recognizes here an inverted idealism, particularly in regards the state of virginity. Pornography is typically puritanical about the virgin state. Women are presumed (for very suspicious reasons) to be better than human, and the hymen is proof of this — they emerge from the creator's hands clean, pure, factory-sealed as it were. Being human, woman naturally do not long remain in this state, to the chagrin of romantically-minded males. Since they are no longer pure they must then be made completely impure. Thus it is that women who naturally, humanly, warmly acknowledge their emotional needs are regarded as vicious.

Men who so acknowledge their needs are, of course, not. It is here, in this rigid belief in the double-standard which it either observes or creates, that the hypocrisy of the eroduction is greatest. It would follow, then, that man in the throes of passion is always somehow noble; that the women, in the same situation, is always ignoble.

This curiously inverted, perhaps even oddly chivalric but certainly unrealistic attitude, is visible even in the ways in which love scenes are photographed. The woman is often completely nude and is observed as an hysterical animal. The man, on the other hand, is always at least partially clothed and, thus appearing in the raiments of civilization, he does not suffer common nudity. While she screams, kicks, and in general abandons herself, he remains thoughtful, calm, a dedicated craftsman.

Her focus of interest is upon the loins, both his and her own. His, however, is upon the breasts and much footage is expanded on scenes of their being caressed and aroused. This reinforces the idea of the man as being above it all (in both senses of the word) and, since he is therefore not directly involved in the essentials of the act, he appears disinterested, civilized, somehow a nobler person than she. He is immune to the vagaries of undisciplined emotion (all women are latent lesbians, homosexuality among men is unknown), to the tyranny of jaded palate (scenes of simulated fellatio are very common, scenes of equally simulated cunnilingus extremely rare), and in all ways displays that he is, obviously, a much better person.

He also displays — and this is something which the eroduction-makers do not intend — an extremely immature relationship with women. Precisely, he reenacts the mother-child relationship. Mother is cast as bad-woman; bad-woman is cast as mother. Even in those scenes where the suspended and unfortunate girl is about to be tortured, there are ritual breast fondlings which would seem to indicate a male attitude extremely ambivalent.

One might simplify and say that if the man with the whip shows the average eroduction customer himself as he would like to be, the same man kneeling in near-adoration before the breasts show him as he truly is. To insist upon this, however, would not explain why Japanese eroductions are really, if unconsciously, concerned with depicting a love-hate relationship of major proportions.

The hatred takes the form of undisguised sadism. The hero has turned his neurosis into a perversion and while this may be more healthy for him, it offers no help to the audience. At the same time, anyone engaging in active sadism is, among other things, proclaiming a profoundly felt inadequacy. The impotence-syndrome observed in some of these pictures supports and explains, on a plot-level at any rate, this inadequacy. At the same time there is ample reason everywhere to see this sadism as merely inverted masochism. Just as idealism is plainly inverted in these pictures to create the universal bad woman, so natural masochism is also inverted to create these endless torture scenes which presumably so engage the audience.

It is presumed that the audiences are engaged or else they would not be in theater. Yet, one might also ask if they are not merely enduring rather than enjoying such savage spectacles in an effort to extract a mite of titillation. In other words, are we not seeing the fantasy of the jaded eroduction executive, rather than viewing an anthropologically interesting attitude on the part of the average eroduction-goer?

That the eroduction fills a social need, no matter how poorly, is beyond doubt. During the few decades during which they have been made in any number, the audience has remained. And, though the films may sometimes resemble the soft-core quickies shown on Times Square or the naughty-nudies shown in Soho, the differences are at once apparent. Those foreign pictures are often little comedies, little melodramas. Innocent of overtone, happy to display the allowed quotient of female flesh, they babble their way to the final reel, mindless and ephemeral. The Japanese eroduction, on the other hand, can be seen as tortured, dark, involved — plainly of psychological import.

The eroduction-makers could claim that I delve too deeply, that their hour-long fantasies were never intended to bear the weight of investigation. And, as for the excessive scenes of torture, well, you have to have some kind of story, and you cannot have plot without good, strong conflict. We make an honest living, they would tell me, because we give our public what it wants. That the public always wants a cheap, safe thrill is their contention, and this, they claim, is all that the eroduction provides.

I would maintain that it provides considerably more. That it, in fact, provides an outlet for the often stultified animosity which all men everywhere must feel toward women from time to time. It expresses this in second-hand terms which, precisely because they do not arouse the intelligence, are potent indeed in arousing and exhausting the emotions. This is because they are dealing with archetypal situations, the essence of the eroduction myth. Like most formula film, the eroduction is also mythic cinema. In these theaters one may go and see a common fantasy endlessly repeated.

This repetition must reassure at least some members of the audience because the fantasy is an infantile one. That woman is an enemy is a sensation that all men have experienced, but it is not one that we usually or necessarily believe. We may cast woman in this role but we do not long keep her there. Yet this is precisely what the eroduction does. With a truly compulsive insistence, it monomaniacally maintains that the nursery vision is the only one, that women are evil, that men are their prey, and that sex is their instrument.

A too cursory glance at the films might seem otherwise — it is the women after all who are being beaten and shoe-horned. Actually, however, prolonged viewing indicates that the tortures

almost invariably result from fear felt by the men. They are doing
in the women before the women have a chance to do them in.
That this is an extremely primitive view of the male-female relationship is obvious, but it is as basic as it is barbaric. It lurks in the
mind of every man and only his knowledge and love and goodwill
can bridge this gap to make happy relations between the sexes
possible at all. This is matched by a fear within the woman herself
and it is her trust and self-knowledge which completes the bridge
connecting her and a man. The eroduction, however, is not concerned with happy relations. Indeed, it does not believe in
them. It encourages in the spectator a rigid dichotomy of thought
and offers ample provocation to every latent love-hate neurosis in
the theater.

Which is perhaps why the eroduction cannot afford to be
human, altruistic, fair-minded. Every speech, every action must
be instantly and compulsively related back to woman's voracious
sexual appetite. In an eroduction even a remark about the weather
carries innuendo. One is caught in a changeless, catatonic state
where each action springs but from one cause, where everyone is
caught, fixed forever, by one's ambivalent sexuality. It is a world
where generosity, freedom, love is unknown. This is the world of
the solitary, the domain of the voyeur.

Naturally, the eroduction is, like all pornographic productions,
masturbatory cinema. The audience is not thinking about
women, it is thinking about itself. The most elemental of fantasies
being acted before it, it is caught, trapped in its own elemental
and hence infantile nature.

In Japan the eroduction seems to be a habit, like smoking,
drinking, biting the nails. Its gratifications are instant, mean-

ingless, and necessary. Quite accidentally and even now unknowingly, the makers of eroductions have tapped an audience of great financial potential. For this reason the films can afford to be shoddy, badly done, unerotic to an extreme, and often ludicrously inept. The economic phenomenon is firmly based upon the psychological phenomenon. The eroduction theater in this sense shares much with the bar and the race-track.

And, like these male retreats, it is essentially harmless. Working out a fantasy never caused anyone any trouble. But, at the same time, the patrons of the eroductions must receive some rather strange ideas of the world they live in — because the point about fantasy is that the real world is, after all, different.

— 1972

A Definition of the Japanese Film

I AM SOMETIMES asked to describe Japanese cinema briefly, to define its essence in a few words. This is impossible. It takes more than a sentence or a paragraph to describe the Japanese film; as I have discovered, it takes entire books. Still, certain general observations may be made: for example, if American cinema is basically about action, and European cinema is basically about character, then Japanese cinema is basically about atmosphere. By this I do not mean that all Japanese films share one particular tone, or elicit the same emotional response. I mean that they often display that heightened sense of reality, which we may call atmosphere.

Before going on to explain how Japanese directors create atmosphere, however, there are certain distinctions to be made between Japanese and Western culture; these distinctions are important because they contribute to vastly different attitudes toward cinema and cinematic technique.

Japanese philosophic tradition sees the individual as an integral part of his world; each man is an extension of the universe.

Western philosophic tradition views the individual as unique, each man being the center of his personal universe.

Nature is complementary to the individual, and one should live in harmony with it.

Nature is an enemy to be conquered, to be used violently if necessary.

Things as they are, are the way things should be. Unhap-

Things as they are, are to be denied; one must always create

py events are simply accepted because they exist. Japanese art observes *mono no aware*, the transience of all earthly things, a concept popularized by Buddhism and of great importance in any discussion of Japanese aesthetics; it implies not only an acceptance of evanescence but also a mild celebration of that very quality.

The Japanese recognizes his dual nature; he is an individual but he is also a social unit in society. If he must choose between his loyalty to himself and his society, he often sacrifices the former.

The Japanese is limited by his attitude. He finds the average, the normal, even the mediocre reassuring.

The Japanese finds in nature, in his social duties, a sense of belonging to something larger than himself, which paradoxically affirms him as an individual.

In the cinema this creates a

a better world where things are as they should be.

The Western individual likes to think of himself as a unique personality, not as part of a larger unit. If he must sacrifice his social persona he gladly does so, since such an action affirms his individuality.

The Westerner strives to exceed limitations. He dislikes the average, the mediocre.

The Westerner, with only his idea of himself to sustain him soon falls into cynicism, into disillusion, into various form of heroics.

In the cinema this creates a

feeling for actuality, since the Japanese accept, although perhaps unwillingly the way things naturally are — thus the sense of realism in the Japanese film.

The films are contemplative and fairly slow. They are rambling stories, built like the Japanese house or garden.

The Japanese realize that the only reality is surface reality. They have no sense of hidden reality, no sense of conscience. They are a people without private guilt, though they do have social shame.

This results in films which do not usually contain any strong personal statements, but which do examine the world in precise detail.

feeling for action, because things as they are cannot be accepted. Films are more concerned with plot than with atmosphere or realistic detail.

The films are filled with action and move very quickly. They are tightly plotted, utilitarian, like the American home or skyscraper.

The West refuses to believe that surface reality is the only reality. For this reason Western religions suggest after-life and stress private conscience. Westerners have little sense of social shame but a great sense of private guilt.

This results in films which are strong personal statements but stress little of the world's realistic detail.

These distinctions are directly related to the matter of cinematic atmosphere. The Japanese director creates atmosphere primarily by limiting his locale; although certain movies produced in the West explore a restricted space, there are many more such films in

Japan. Naruse's *Sounds from the Mountain (Yama no Oto)*, takes place entirely within one house, with occasional shots of the street outside; Gosho's *An Inn in Osaka (Osaka no Yado)* likewise shows a small inn and its environs, while Ozu's *Tokyo Story (Tokyo Monogatari)* examines two houses. Kurosawa's *Red Beard (Akahige)*, Imai's *Night-Drum (Yoru no Tsuzumi)*, and Kobayashi's *Hara-Kiri (Seppuku)* all show neighborhoods dominated by single buildings: a hospital, a samurai's house, a lord's mansion. Shindo's *The Island (Hadaka no Shima)* takes place on an island, while Oshima's *Death by Hanging (Koshukei)* is confined to a death cell and its imaginary extensions. Whether the chosen space is exterior or interior, however, it is always treated as an integral, tightly controlled unit.

The use of restricted space is more than a technical characteristic, however. It reflects the Japanese inclination toward indirect expression. In Toyoda's *A Tale from East of the Sumida River (Bokutokidan)* the action all takes place in Fujiko Yamamoto's house, except for a few shots of the streets outside and a neighboring house. Toyoda chooses to narrate a simple story with virtually no plot: his attention is entirely directed to character development, and, practicing oblique expression, he uses the house as an extension of its master. During the course of this two-hour film we come to know the house intimately, upstairs and down; as its presence becomes familiar its owner becomes familiar by association. The increment of realistic detail within a well-defined space establishes an atmosphere, which in turn creates a character; Fujiko Yamamoto becomes credible indirectly, by means of a totally believable realistic atmosphere.

Japanese cinema is based on the concept that less means more.

The less a director shows, the more carefully he must choose what he does show. Though Kurosawa is not considered by the Japanese to be particularly representative of Japanese culture, compare his *The Lower Depths (Donzoko)* with that of Jean Renoir *(Les Basfonds)*. Kurosawa's film is made of so much less — a house, the people living in it, the yard outside, the sky above. Renoir is most interested in character, in closeups of Louis Jouvet, of Jean Gabin. Kurosawa uses few closeups in his film. Rather we see his characters in groups of two or three, and always framed by the house, which is in every scene. Renoir takes us outside, Kurosawa keeps us inside. In all, Kurosawa shows us less, but his film implies more and demands more.

The spectator, presented with less than he perhaps expected, must bring more of himself to the film, must allow himself to think and feel more. He is like a lens: the less light there is, the more he must open himself. When Antonioni discovered this in *L'Avventura* and presented long scenes with "nothing" in them, it was hailed in the West as a major aesthetic discovery; and so it was, in the West. But the Japanese film and Japanese audiences had long understood the principle of understatement.

Igor Stravinsky once said that until he knew how long a piece of music should be, and until he knew its instrumentation, he could not begin to write. Without these restrictions he could not compose. "This is true freedom," he said. "All the freedom in the world means nothing to me." Japanese cinema affirms Stravinsky's theory; its essence is restriction. Yasujiro Ozu has said that he writes his scripts with certain actors in mind: if he did not he could not write, any more than a painter could paint if he did not know what colors he was to use.

There are various ways for the director to restrict, and consequently amplify, his film. He may limit his locale, his theme, or his method of description. Kenji Mizoguchi's method of creating atmosphere depends entirely on two limits: he puts the action far from the camera and continues the scene for a long time. These two restrictions are seen, for example, in the lawn scene from *Ugetsu*. Machiko Kyo and Masayuki Mori are in the far distance playing on the grass by the shores of Lake Biwa. Nothing happens, yet the scene continues for some time. The result is that we slowly absorb the beauty of the scene and, consequently, apprehend what the surroundings mean to the two in the far distance. We feel the atmosphere much as they themselves feel it. By giving us almost nothing to look at, Mizoguchi has led us to see.

Although the film no longer exists, Eizo Tanaka's 1917 version of Tolstoy's *The Living Corpse (Ikeru Shikabane)* was an example of the use of atmosphere as limitation. In this film, nature becomes a generalized substitute for specific emotion. When the director used the closeup, he did not use it, as Western directors almost invariably do, to illustrate an emotional climax: he used it directly before that climax. At the emotional zenith — the heroine receives some bad news — he pulled back and showed her alone in a field, leaning against a tree. In other words, just where the West would have called for a closeup to show emotion, the Japanese director made the barren field, the lonely tree, the cloudy sky comment upon the emotional state of the heroine. This is the Japanese way of seeing, of showing things. Forty years later, in *The Throne of Blood (Kumo no Su-jo)*, Kurosawa again deliberately pulled back his camera at the emotional height of the story. When

Toshiro Mifune finally realizes the worst, when Isuzu Yamada feels most strongly, the camera retreats. We see their emotion from a proper distance, framed by clouded skies and an encroaching castle.

The later films of Yasujiro Ozu offer particularly good examples of the Japanese genius for meaningful restriction. The camera is stationary, and there is virtually no punctuation save that of the straight cut. In Ozu's pictures it becomes impossible not to bring oneself into his milieu; the spectator is totally involved in a carefully controlled vision of house and family. Such involvement is virtually unavoidable in his films, not only because Ozu creates a totally credible atmosphere, but also because he understands the basic nature of film. The cinema's greatest strength is that it is able to record perfectly the surface of life, nothing more. Since this is so, we should expect no more than a reflection of surface reality; the first films were newsreels and every film remains, in essence, a newsreel. Those great closeups of emotionally contorted faces in Western cinema and in some Japanese films as well do not usually make us feel grief, pain, or happiness; what those images really convey are skin pores, mascara, and nostril hair.

Since cinematic art, however, is symbolic, we accept this cosmeticized monster face as a representation of human emotion; we accept it even though we are not necessarily convinced by it. But when Ozu shows us Setsuko Hara at the end of *Late Autumn (Akibiyori)* sitting alone in the middle distance, hands folded, eyes downcast, we move nearer and nearer to a genuine feeling of sadness. One of the reasons is that Ozu does not demand our emotions and, paradoxically, we more freely give them. But the most important reason is that by showing in the way he does, by respecting the surface appearance of life, he succeeds in suggesting the depths beneath the surface. He allows us to apprehend the emotional quality of life which its surface — that portion captured by the camera — can only suggest. The less he shows, the more we feel. In doing this he respects not only us and himself, he respects the very nature of cinema.

The Japanese director could not respect the nature of cinema unless he also respected the nature of life itself. His aim, like that of all film directors, is complete credibility, but the Japanese director is better equipped than most to achieve this end. We have already seen that he uses the atmosphere of a place to ensure our belief in it, that he purposely restricts what he shows and how he shows it to ensure our participation. Now we shall see the respect that the Japanese has for life, and consequently for cinema.

Several years ago I watched some workmen building a new wall where I lived in Azabu. Nearby was a tree with low-hanging branches. The workmen continued to build the wall and it rose closer and closer to the lowest branch. They stopped, talked, then continued building. They built a hole in the wall to accommodate the branch. They did not cut off the branch as the Westerner would, as the Japanese probably would today; they enriched their wall with it.

Again the filmic example must be Ozu. The typical Ozu scene begins rather briskly and the story is forwarded a shot or two. Then, after this is finished, at the very point where the Western director would cut the film, one character turns to another and remarks about the weather, pauses to wonder about something, or simply sits and looks. The camera regards this, recording it;

sound stops, movement ceases. It is a moment of silence, of repose before the next scene. These tiny empty moments are the pores in an Ozu picture, through which the movie breathes; they define the film by their emptiness. They are examples of *mu*, a Zen aesthetic term implying, among other things, nothingness; they are also examples of care and respect. Compare this to the somewhat ruthless manner of the average Western director. He would have ended the scene after the plot had been forwarded, as though plot and not people was what he was really interested in. And in so doing he would have missed the most meaningful portion of the scene.

One of the strengths of traditional Japanese cinema lies in its refusal to depend on plot. To define plot one might turn to the late E.M. Forster's celebrated definition: the king died and then the queen died is a story; the queen died because the king died is a plot. The story reflects simple reality; the plot comments upon that reality, ascribing motives and relating actions. Plot cannot, however, be the business of cinema, which must always concern itself with recording surface reality. The aim of cinematic art is to take life as it is and to pattern it in some way which does not do violence to its nature. Plot is a pattern which does violence; it demands action and events, as opposed to the increment of precise surface detail, thus changing the nature of film as recorder of visible reality.

The Japanese have restored some of the realistic basis of cinema by emphasizing story rather than plot. This emphasis reflects Japanese literature, in which many classical situations are based on *giri-ninjo*, or obligation versus inclination. The resolution of this simple opposition takes the place of a complex plot. Furthermore,

Japanese literary history favors epic narrative: *The Tale of Ise* and *The Tale of Genji* are long chronicles in which events follow one another in episodic sequence. In this tradition, the first important Japanese film, *Souls on the Road (Rojo no Reikon)*, a 1921 picture by Minoru Murata and Kaoru Osanai, consisted of just two interwoven stories. In their editing, Murata and Osanai were not interested in contrasting thoughts and ideas, but in creating parallels of feeling and atmosphere. Their two stories were not dissimilar to begin with, and the directors emphasized similarity rather than difference. Griffith's *Way Down East*, a heavily plotted melodrama with a strong theatrical sense of form, made at approximately the same time, exemplifies the distinction between Japanese and Western attitudes toward film. The difference in narrative structure is also reflected in the difference between formalized Western endings and Japanese endings. Unlike *Way Down East, Souls on the Road* simply stops; it has no formal conclusion. Although Japanese cinema has probably as many unhappy formal endings as the cinema of the West has happy ones, it also has a large number of informal, or open-ended, conclusions. These endings actually conclude nothing and are the proper choice in films which reflect the rhythms of existence: life itself never ends in any particularly meaningful manner. Happy or unhappy endings belong only to plotted films, which tie up life in a neat package; the happy ending is the bow on the top. Story, on the other hand, needs no such conclusion; it merely stops after a certain number of episodes. Like *Souls on the Road*, the best films of Ozu, Naruse, Shimazu, Toyoda, and Gosho have no endings. There is a pause in the story, a pause in the lives of the characters, and instead of the next episode we see the announcement, "The End."

Film takes time to make its full impression and, until recently, the Japanese were almost alone in recognizing this. The length of Japanese films still causes complaint in the hurried West; even Pudovkin once said that there was "too much unnecessary footage" in Japanese films. But time is always used for a purpose — to make one feel. One remembers what Mizoguchi said: put the action at a distance from the camera and make the scene last a long time. There are other ways of making long sequences, however, and here Japanese editing differs from Western editing: it intensifies atmosphere. One excellent example of such editing is a sequence from Ozu's 1949 picture *Late Spring (Banshun)* which best typifies the subtlety and restraint of Japanese cinema. Ozu wanted to show the daughter (Setsuko Hara) becoming aware of the interest her father (Chishu Ryu) supposedly has in marrying Kuniko Miyake. As some very delicate feelings are involved, Ozu did not wish to use dialogue — rightly, he wanted to show rather than state. He chose to set the scene at a Noh drama performance and the only sound during this sequence is the sound of the Noh itself. The sequence runs this way:

Middle-shot of Hara and Ryu at the theater watching the
  Noh
The Noh play itself
Long-shot of the audience including Hara and Ryu
Closeup of Ryu's pleased face
Middle-shot of the actors in the Noh, the main actor, etc.
Middle-shot of the second actor and the chorus
Middle-shot of Hara and Ryu
The Noh play

Middle-shot of the actors
Long-shot of the Noh play
Ryu: he bows to someone
Hara: she looks, then nods
Miyake: she bows in return
Hara and Ryu: she turns to look at her father
Miyake watching the play
Hara, her eyes downcast
Middle-shot of Hara and Ryu
Closeup of Hara, again looking at Ryu
Closeup of Ryu, pleased with the play
Closeup of Hara, sad
Closeup of Miyake watching the play
Closeup of Hara, sadder
Long-shot of the audience including Hara and Ryu
Long-shot of the play
Closeup of Hara, sad, bowing her head
A tree in the wind, the music of the Noh continuing

This is one of the most beautifully edited sequences in all Japanese cinema. It runs approximately three minutes and is completely economical. Ozu used twenty-six separate cuts to achieve the effect he wanted, and there is not one wasted moment; each scene follows the next with perfect visual logic. In the West, the sequence would probably be done in about five shots, one for each character and one or two for the play itself. The central point, that Setsuko Hara doesn't want her father to marry, would be made rapidly, and we would be rushed to the next sequence. By the end of the film we would probably forget the entire incident, or remember it only as a plot complication. The sequence in *Late Spring*, however, is unforgettable. The reason is, of course, Ozu's technique. He added cut after cut as a painter would apply brush strokes, each one contributing to the final impression. Ozu edited not to contrast scenes but to compare them, to create an incremental structure in which the scenes sustain one another. In so doing he created a feeling of actuality, he forwarded his story, and he took the amount of time necessary for us both to be convinced of what was happening, and to apprehend emotionally the impact of the event on the heroine. Finally, but perhaps most important, by creating that final image of the tree in the wind over the Noh music he created a rare conjunction of a physical with a spiritual state.

I have discussed only a fraction of Japanese cinema. There is far more to be said, and many exceptions to be made to my remarks. For every Ozu there are dozens of Japanese directors who neither know nor care about the nature of cinema. *An Inn in Osaka* is opposed to hundreds of Japanese movies which respect reality no more than does the average California or Cinecitta production. Furthermore, there are other more objectionable qualities of the Japanese film which I have not mentioned: the typical reliance on the overly explanatory, for example; the presence of the *benshi* or the lecturer — commentator of the silent period, which still influences cinema; the shameless exploitation of sentimentality for its own sake which ruins many pictures, including those of Gosho, Toyoda, Kurosawa.

Moreover, the virtues I have been describing have now vanished from the Japanese film as they are vanishing from Japanese life. Where there is no more *shomin* (the lower-middle class) there can be no more *shomin-geki* (films about the lower-middle class). In an affluent society, there is no more *mono no aware*. In a land where little is forbidden, there can be none of the energy or power of restriction. Less still means more, but the Japanese no longer believe it. There are doubtless strong economic reasons for all of this, but the economic explanation, whatever it strength, is never sufficient.

Over thirty-five years ago Junichiro Tanizaki saw what was happening. He wrote of it in his fine essay, *In-ei Raisan* (translated as *In Praise of Shadows*). Japan has chosen to be false to its own history, its own nature, and consequently, its reality has changed. To a certain extent, that is to be expected in any modern industrial nation. But Japan's attitude toward reality has truly altered. In a land where nature is no longer respected, where today is seen in terms of tomorrow, the regard for truth which creates art can no longer exist. Everything I have indicated about the Western film may now be applied, with equal accuracy, to contemporary Japanese film. Japan, the first country to understand the true nature of cinema, has now seemingly lost that ability.

Remember the final shot of *Late Spring*. It is the sea. We have only seen the sea once, as a background, during the entire film. In the final scene we watch Chishu Ryu come home after his daughter's wedding. He is alone now. He picks up an pear and begins to peel it. We see his face. He is a man alone, and he is accepting his situation. Then comes the final cut to the rolling sea. Ozu has shown us a particular man and then he shows us the sea, the symbol of permanent change. Far from being surprised, we are reassured because Ozu has shown us the truth of human life.

He has created a film which shows us the world as it is. He accepts it, and ultimately, through his intervention, so do we.

—1970

VI

TV: The Presentational Image

TELEVISION PRESENTS only itself and it presents itself as only television. The convention of theater, of film, is that something else is being presented — life itself. And this is also the convention of certain elements of television — the drama, the movie — but the format of the media, that of a day-long, night-long variety show, prevents its pretending to be anything other than what it is. This being so, presentation in television is direct. The person doing the talking looks directly at us, the watchers. There is no convention to insist that we are looking at something other than what we are. They only reality is the ostensible — someone in front of the TV camera talking to us.

If we are being addressed this directly by commentator or by salesman, we are, in a way, also addressing them. These people are doing it *for* us, the watchers, and our opinion of them is for various reasons valuable. They want to appear at their best both because they wish to sell us something or influence us in some other way and because, since they are in the public eye, they want in more general terms our good opinion. Various are the ways in which they attempt to obtain this.

We are all familiar with many of the means — carefully chosen words, an implied flattery, the attempt to create enthusiasm, a certain ingratiating unnatural naturalness. We are not so familiar (nor are they) with less conscious means: those through which they, perhaps unknowingly, imply and we, often equally unknowingly, infer; those through which we consciously deduce. These would include what they say without using words — the speech of the face, the hands, the stance; it would also include their ideas on the medium and how to use it, ideas we deduce from viewing TV as an entirety; it would also include their true, rather than their merely stated opinion of us.

Naturally this varies in various countries since assumptions upon which this behavior rests vary conspicuously from one culture to another. This being so, something is revealed about assumptions, beliefs, and generally agreed upon ideas, when these varying positions are regarded. Those to be seen in Japan are common to that country and there are a great many of them.

So many that it is difficult to know where to begin. Let us start with one which is, so far as I know, unique. This consists of the commentator at one side of the small screen and an assistant at the other. The commentator is always male and usually middle-aged. The assistant is always female, usually young and often pretty. He comments on the news or upon the subject of whatever the program is, and she assists.

But her assistance is so minimal that, to our eyes, she might as well not be there at all. Not for her the "equal" participation of the American "anchor person." She nods soberly at the camera when he makes his various pronouncements; she says *So, desu ne?* (Isn't that just true though?) when he makes a cogent point; and she will sometimes add a bit of information of her own which, upon examination, turns out to be a rephrasing of what he himself has just said.

To people of other cultures watching these two the effect is unsettling. We are certainly used to double commentators but usually each commentator really comments. In this format — and it is very common on Japanese television — the pretty girl is not only redundant, she seems absolutely unnecessary. Precisely, we fail to comprehend her function. Yet she has a very important one.

A commentator is, by definition, giving his opinion. In the West this is quite enough. One man's opinion is as good as another's, etc. In Japan, however, to give an opinion is to appear opinionated, and this is a fault in a society where dissenting opinion is at least officially unvoiced, and where a concensus of opinion is the invariable goal. These two qualities are hopefully ensured by this near-mute, if attractive, young lady. Her nods and monosyllables of agreement indicate that he is not alone in his opinion and that therefore he is not merely opinionated. Rather, he is stating a truth, since more than one person agrees upon what he says. At the same time she introduces harmony — it would be unthinkable of her to disagree with him or even to offer a conflicting opinion of her own — by indicating that we *all* (and it is *us* she is so earnestly nodding at) agree and the wished-for consensus has, indeed, already been reached.

One can trace this strange duo back to radio, where they are still to be heard, his voice supported from time to time by her syllables of assent. One can perceive its principles in even earlier forms of entertainment. In the Bunraku doll-drama, the various voices of characters and commentator (all spoken and sung by a single man) are mutually supportive; in the Noh drama, the chorus affirms and comments upon the dialogue. I can think of no instance where the commentary is not supportive, which means that I can think of no example where irony or any other "deeper" meaning is even suggested. Nor should it be, since the intention is a straight presentation within a context which seeks to make us regard the ostensible and only that as the real. This is as true, in

Japan, of ancient drama as it is of modern television. It is, however, only radio and television which has made the assenting voice female, thereby plainly implying that women in Japan have a male-supportive role — and no other.

That women are somehow the weaker sex and are therefore naturally subservient is a typically Japanese message and appears in many forms through many different media. In television this major burden is carried by the commercials where, by implication, the woman is only daughter, wife, homemaker, and mother. In these roles she is identified almost entirely as a consumer: when young she eats chocolates and tries new face creams on camera; married, she is careful about underarm odor and the kind of menstrual napkin she wears; about the house she smiles over the virtues of detergents, air-conditioners, vacuum sweepers, and as a mother she forces various foods on her surprised and delighted spouse and children.

In this, of course, Japanese television is little different from television in any consumer society. The difference is the directness with which this is done. In ostensibly democratic and egalitarian America the commentator's helper would be laughed (if somewhat nervously) off the screen; and any such overt suggestion (there are covert suggestions aplenty) that woman's place is in the home would no longer help sell the product. As always in Japan, however, the intention is so open, so unveiled, so unmarred by any irony or duplicity, that the messages emerge with an often startling clarity.

Take, for example, the "togetherness" that is being pushed by TV commercials now that the "prime selling target" has moved from wife and children, and become the family as a unit. In Japan, it should be understood, to be a family man is a very progressive social stance to take. It means that one is unwilling to sacrifice one's family (and, by extension, oneself) to the all-powerful employer. One's private concerns now come before one's social responsibilities. This mini-revolution is actually meaningless because, in practice, it means that the husband merely devotes more leisure time to his family and may, occasionally, attempt to avoid working at the company on Sundays. But the idea of such a revolution is very attractive. One of the symptoms is the wide use of the English "my" in various slogans: ("My Car/My Family"). It is symptomatic of the symptom that it is the English "my" which is used and not the Japanese *watakushi no*. The one, being a foreign word is as yet free from the unwelcome egotistical nuances which surround the Japanese.

Another symptom is the "happy family" which now finds its way into TV commercials. Here father, mother and kids are all gathered at the family table or, more rarely, on the family *tatami* while mother introduces them to this or that new product. Their glee is so extreme that even father is carried away by it. He compliments his wife on her buying prowess. *Sasuga* ("Isn't that just like her") he says, smacking his lips and beaming. She simpers her pleasure and the children grimace and look at each other knowingly — everything is OK with Mom and Dad.

Messages are rife in this small vignette. Among things suggested are: buying the right things is the true secret of a happy home life, at the same time the wife's role as mere shopper has been subtly reinforced because she is after all fulfilling herself in this role, just look at the smiles on those kids' faces, and just look at the playfull hug her husband is giving her — things are going to be OK in bed tonight too.

There are some perhaps unintended messages as well. The one which strikes me most strongly is the apparent lunacy of the family. They behave like manic-depressives in the upward swing — all those roguish smiles and frenetic laughs over what is, after all, only a new breakfast food or laundry soap. It is the behavior of the mouse family or the rabbit family in the animated cartoons. There is something quite inhuman about these excesses.

Abroad, the TV watcher is, naturally, already familiar with this type of crazy family. He is so familiar with it that he is prepared to read the message with a certain cynicism. When sponsors discovered this, the family was promptly removed — the substitute was another family shifted a few millimeters nearer reality. In Japan, however, the viewer is usually immune to cynicism — being Japanese — and the family is taken at face value. These people are happy with their new product: this is the only message read.

(That the sell is very hard indeed is apparent. But in Japan there is only hard sell — no soft. The reason is that, in a culture where the ostensible is always the real, any attempt at soft sell — and there have been some — results in an unfortunate side-effect: the sponsor doesn't really believe in his product; he is sneaky and shifty in its presentation; if it is good enough to buy why doesn't he just say so?)

More important than this simple reading, however, is what the reading affirms. In being happy with the new product the family has reached yet further agreement, yet higher harmony. No dissent, no confrontation will rend this happy group. And by behaving like a demented mouse-family this social unit has, furthermore, shown that they are unexceptionable, that they are Mr. and Mrs. Status Quo with all their little Quos — that they are, in fact, no threat.

I am no threat. This message is so clear and so incessant on Japanese television, and so accounts for the tone of the medium, that one must examine the phenomenon in some detail.

One might begin by noticing that the adults in TV commercials are all really children. They cock their heads like precocious youngsters, they use the gestures of the school-child, they smile and laugh in the most uninhibited manner (and one markedly in contrast to the smiles and laughter of true Japanese adults), and cajole in a way truly typical of the spoiled Japanese child. Further, the disembodied voices in these commercials (those we listen to while looking at the products) are plainly adults imitating children. Further yet, the music accompanying all this is reminiscent of the jaunty marches associated, in Japan at any rate, with kindergarten.

Perhaps behind all of this is some urge to return to the golden age of undisciplined, permissive, Japanese childhood, but the implication (to the extent that any is acknowledged) would seem to be that we are all as harmless as children. Look at us: we make fools of ourself, we invite you to laugh at us, we are fatuous to a degree — and yet, since we are so harmless, your laughter cannot but be indulgent, your hand cannot but reach into your pocket, your fingers cannot but open up the billfold. And if you don't want to — then no harm done because, you see, we have really asked for nothing.

In a way this is soft-sell with a vengeance. These monstrous children are, in a truly childlike manner, having it both ways at once. It is in this manner that their message reaches the consumer who, not having been really, truly asked, can feel all the more free to do just what has been suggested. The happy family has merely offered him an example of unexceptionable, non-threatening togetherness.

Look how unexceptionable I am: this is a message which demotes the threat of another person looking into your living room, and if the actors in TV commercials purposely imitate children, those non-pros on the talk-shows, the amateur hours, the endless "personal" interviews, indicate that the childplay is based upon something very real.

Notice the hands of the ordinary citizen when he appears on television — and bear in mind that in Japan the ordinary citizen is brought to appear on the tube with a frequency greater, I would guess, than in any other country. Where are the hands? They are folded in front of him, one gripping the other, in the lap if he is sitting, at the crotch if he is standing. This is the "good" position.

On foreign TV, particularly American, the non-pro often seeks to make something of his personality by waving his hands about more than he ordinarily would. They suddenly become "expressive" of him. Likewise, his stance — if he is standing — is not that of the ordinary Japanese facing the TV camera. He will assume a "natural" stance, in which the pelvis is expressively tilted — just a hint of aggression. If he stood as does his opposite Japanese number, feet together, hands safely in front, something like the schoolboy at attention, Americans would read the image as indication of embarrassment, would see someone who is immature, and, at any rate, someone without "an outgoing personality."

But in Japan, conversely, the gesticulating foreigner is seen as egotistical (a bad thing), ill-mannered, and quite capable of disturbing an implied social harmony by his individualistic gesturing. On the other hand, the Japanese are all standing in well-mannered identical positions (well-mannered, to an extent, because they *are* identical), no one calling any undue attention to himself, all possible areas of danger (the hands, the pelvis) under firm control, all individualistic tendencies properly sacrificed to attain a goal of unexceptionable "good manners" — how well brought-up, how proper they indeed are.

(Apparent contradictions to these observations are, I think, only apparent. That Japanese TV dramas, differentiated from the commercials, are filled with the utmost anti-social violence does not indicate that such a display is to be condoned. Rather, it indicates a concern for the natural violence which hands firmly in the lap keep successfully under control. It is part titillation and part horrible example — in any event those exhibiting this degree of individuality are always reformed, put into prison, or killed. In the same way, the fact that in the home-dramas the happy housewife is revealed to be a mass of suffering, given to multiple love affairs, abortions, ungrateful children and a high degree of suicide, indicates no further degree of reality about real Japanese housewives. Rather, it represents an opposite extreme — both ends being equally far from middle : the real Japanese woman. In any event, both violence and tear-jerking are illustrations of fantasies entertained by sponsors and TV producers, if not by the audience.)

The pervading juvenility of Japanese TV is the result of its conciliatory intentions. The complete fatuity of all Japanese programing except the dramas (where the fatuousness is of a different degree), its bland, inane foolishness, is a small price to pay when the result if something as grand as complete uniformity and utter consistency. Still, to the foreign viewer, Japanese television brings to mind Douglas MacArthur's famous (and much resented) description of the Japanese as a nation of twelve year-olds. It also makes one think that the general missed the age by at least a decade.

I am not saying that the Japanese are really like this. I am saying that the image they project on television, the image they choose to present is precisely this. One sees it in other situations. (Japanese formal behavior — so relentlessly conciliatory — remains absurd to foreigners who do not understand its reasons.) These are always those where a degree of presentation is called for. We are unexceptionable, we are no threat, we are — just look — nice and good. An evening of Japanese TV — in which this single intention is tirelessly presented and represented — makes one wonder just how the myth of Japanese inscrutability ever got started : could anything be simpler, or more simple-minded, than this open, naked display?

What we are seeing, however, is only that which has been selected. People on the tube — pro and amateur alike, both the newscasters and those who design the commercial — select (telling word) their "image." Just as the Americans choose to present a type which is more individual, more argumentative, more "vital," than anyone you are apt to find on an American street-corner, so the Japanese have chosen an image carefully lacking in any obvious individuality, given wholeheartedly to assent, but equally "vital" in that the goal of the presentation is a uniform front. That safety would be identified with childishness, and security with inanity are natural consequences of the presentational aim. Here too, as in the dramas, we are dealing in part with hopeful fantasy — since no people could ever be as bland nor as unexceptional as those on Japanese TV. Unlike the fantasy in the dramas, however, this is accepted as "real." One presents this image as into a reflecting mirror. And that mirror is the audience.

— 1980

Mizushobai: The Art of Pleasing

VISITORS TO JAPAN are impressed not only by the social order and the cultural beauty of the country, they also remark most favorably upon the quality of the service. Waiters perform with a willing alacrity unknown in other lands, bar hostesses are solicitous to a degree foreign to the rest of the world, elevator girls bow to everyone, and the geisha, as is well known, have transformed ingratiating service into a high art — the art of pleasing.

In the West one hears of the customer being always right, though he somehow never seems to be. In Japan, on the other hand, he definitely is. Almost any request is promptly gratified and a waiter has never been known to say: "Sorry, this isn't my table." Even the unruly customer is right. The bartender will accept an insult with a smile, the waitress accommodates public rudeness with affability, and no one, from the taxi driver up — or down — expects a tip.

It seems, to the first-time visitor at any rate, as though the art of pleasing is for its own sake — as though one portion of the population has elected to devote itself to creating a sense of powerful well-being in the other portion, and all for no ostensible extra reward. In Japan one is treated not only to superb service but also service with a perfectly sincere smile.

This fact has much intrigued foreign visitors and has long taken its place among the mysteries of inscrutable Japan. Actually, however, there is nothing mysterious about it. The life of service has a venerable history in Japan and the attitudes proper to it have long been codified. An understanding of how it works, and what it means, demands only that one sees the phenomenon from the Japanese point of view.

Japan, a country given to categorizing, traditionally divides its working force into two parts. The numerically larger half comprises the professions, white and blue collar alike, and all the crafts and industries attendant upon them. This half is sometimes — and in contradistinction to the other half — characterized as *katai shobai* or, as we might paraphrase it, "steady work." The second half is given over to the service professions — and these include those occupations which, for various reasons, katai shobai finds unsteady: actors, waiters, musicians, most of the traditionally female professions from coffee-shop girl to geisha, and many, many more. This kind of work is called *mizushobai*, literally, "water work," the implication being that these occupations are fluid, formless, unstable as water itself. The terms have further nuances as well: katai shobai is considered respectable work; thus, by definition, mizushobai is not considered proper or fitting; it can even be disreputable. The man who drops out of the company in order to open a snack bar has committed an act close to social indecency.

Given this attitude one might wonder what attractions the mizushobai life could have for its members. Actually, the attractions are considerable. Decent, hardworking Japan is so very *katai* (this time in the word's other sense of being hard and unyielding) that the rat-race, rabbit-hutch life, no matter how respectable, begins to lose its value.

The very fluidity of the mizushobai life is thus one of its major appeals. One works as one likes, one takes time off as one can afford to, one no longer has a big-brother company looking over the shoulder demanding a proper attitude — proper marriage, proper children, proper schools to send them to. In a sense mizushobai is a vast ghetto, and in this context ghetto life is attractive.

Certainly, also, the world of the mizushobai offers occupations to millions who, underprivileged in various ways, cannot find proper and fitting work. In particular, women who want to work have no place else to go; professional women are a token minority in Japan and even then they are expected to make the daily tea for the office, in itself a mizushobai-like undertaking. How much more attractive the life of a bar hostess is, where one can make in only one evening as much as during a month in the office and all without — contrary to public opinion — having to please to the *full* extent of the customer's wishes.

The unmindful assumptions of the respectable public, and even the occasional insult is a small price indeed for mizushobai folk to pay for the freedom and — once one is in the upper reaches of this work — the monetary rewards of those professions. (The lower reaches are not too rewarding.) If one owns a lucrative bar or snack shop, if one becomes a famous screen or TV entertainer, the rewards are great and the public's attitude not too difficult to bear.

In addition, the mizushobai professionals, like the medieval guild members they resemble, have their own ways of being decent and taking a proper pride in their work. Tips are never demanded and are accepted only in return for extraordinary services — the porter who has had to go all the way to the station for one's trunk, or the geisha who, having received four fur coats and two convertibles, decides to give in.

Mizushobai thus offers the hardworking Japanese an alternative to the big-business style of life that is rapidly becoming ubiquitous. In this it is no different from what it has always been. The "willow world" of the Tokugawa period with its actors and wrestlers and courtesans and palanquin bearers was much the same and performed the same services.

Mizushobai remains a way out of the samurai/businessman life and, at the same time, offers the means to a well-paying profession. The art of pleasing, with its own standards, its own integrity, lives on.

—1981

The Japanese Kiss

MORE THAN 100 years ago, May 31, 1883, to be exact, the brothers Goncourt wrote in their journal that dinner conversation had been about kissing and that "somebody who had lived for many years in Japan said that the kiss did not exist in Japanese love-making." This early, then, the West knew of Japan's odd relation to the kiss.

Nowadays, of course, Japan is full of it. Just look around — billboards, magazines, TV itself, lots of kissing . . . and more. But this was not always so and even now the kiss in Japan does not quite means what it does in the West.

To begin with, there wasn't any kissing — at least, not officially. In Japan, as in China, the kiss was invisible. Lovers never kissed in public; family members never kissed. The touching of the lips never became the culturally encoded action it has for so long been in Europe and America.

Nonetheless, some people kissed. One knows this from the erotic prints. Yet, even here, the full kiss is rare. It is almost as though it were an occasional practice, a further perversion, rather than the standard fare it is in the West. Certainly, it was something one did only when carried away by passion itself. And, of a consequence, the kiss remained only, singularly, sexual.

Imagine then the surprise felt by early Japanese abroad who found mothers kissing children and fathers kissing mothers, and all in public. Yukichi Fukuzawa, the later statesman and educator, in the United States in 1860 as a member of the retinue of the Shogun's envoy, has mentioned this surprise in his journals.

As befits a statesman and diplomat, he realized that he was

viewing a cultural aberration. This indiscriminate pressing together of mouths did not shock him. He viewed the odd practice somewhat as Americans of the period were viewing Eskimo nose-rubbing.

At the same time, however, kissing was not among the foreign customs introduced into the rapidly modernizing country. Still, kissing was so much a part of the Western world that it kept intruding itself. For example, in modern novels being translated into Japanese. Donald Keene writes of one such example in the early translation of Bulwer-Lytton's *Ernest Maltravers* — fittingly Japanized as *A Springtime Tale of Blossoms and Willows.*

In it the hero speaks of his satisfaction "if I could get one kiss from those coral lips." This the translator, doubtless after some thought, translated as "if I could get one lick of your red lips." Though there existed in the new dictionaries a word for "kiss," the translator preferred *hitoname* (literally, "one lick"), doubtless feeling that licking was, after all, a more decent activity than kissing.

In the event, Alice, she of the coral lips, "hid her face with her hands." In Japanese, however, Arisu "hid her face with her sleeve and though she would speak could find no words," so affected was she by what had nearly transpired.

Though the practice of kissing doubtless continued in private, its appearance in public remained condemned. It was even made a statutory offense, punishable by fine or detention if "committed" in public. What outrage had occurred to make such a law necessary is not recorded, but it remained on the books from the early 1920s through 1945, when it was finally rescinded by the Occupation authorities.

While it was in force it was also evoked. There was a famous incident in the 1930s when Rodin's celebrated *Le Baisir* was to be exhibited. This sculpture is of a completely nude couple in the act of kissing. The police promptly prohibited the proposed exhibition.

The Japanese authorities were scandalized that such a thing would be shown; the French authorities were scandalized that it would not be. Diplomatic pressure was brought to bear and the police themselves suggested a solution. As social-critic Kimpei Shiba has told it, the authorities said that the nudity was, of course, permissible — therefore the work might be shown if just the heads were in some way muffled, perhaps if a cloth were wrapped around them.

It was not until after the Pacific War that the Rodin was seen in Japan. Now it is on permanent display, to be seen anytime by anyone, on the plaza in front of the Tokyo Museum of Western Art in Ueno. Its appearance, however, should not be taken as indication that the kiss in Japan has (in Western terms) been entirely normalized.

Indeed, kissing has only with difficulty become even a semi-accepted convention. Take, for example, the difficulties occasioned by its public debut — in the movies.

Before the war, of course, all kissing scenes were routinely cut from foreign films — at great peril to their continuity. Hero and heroine would look deeply into each other's eyes. They would move closer and closer together. Then they would snap apart with a suddenness that ought to have set their teeth rattling.

Now, however, post-1945, with Western ways loose, indeed rampant, within the country, the time of the kiss had come. In

1946 the Daiei Motion Picture Company planned "the first kiss scene in any Japanese film." It was to be included in a picture appropriately named *A Certain Night's Kiss*. At the last moment, however, Daiei lost its nerve. The director made obscure the important event by having his heroine coyly open her umbrella at the crucial point.

The honors consequently went to a Shochiku film, *Twenty Year-Old Youth*, where there was an appropriately shameless kiss, right on the lips. An indication of how little kissing was accepted is seen in the degree of sensation which this osculation occasioned. The press wrote of nothing else. Was this kiss "merely commercial" or was it "artistically motivated"? Was it "hygienic"? Did it have a "sexual motive"? And, was it "Japanese or not"?

No agreement was possible but a majority decided against its being hygienic. For some time after, kiss-scenes were faked, and shot from an angle where the fakery would not be apparent. Or, if that proved impossible, then the principals would wear touched up gauze over the lips for the dirty event.

Even now there is the feeling, in public entertainments at any rate, that the kiss is somehow not entirely Japanese. It is telling that the only thoroughly accepted screen kiss in the postwar era was a "foreign" one. This was in a film called *A Brilliant Revenge*. The long on-screen kiss was occasioned by the performance of a foreign drama. Since all Japanese were pretending to be foreigners it was perfectly proper, in fact in character, for them to spend periods of time with their lips glued to each other.

The discrimination continues. There is, for example, a perfectly good Japanese word for "kiss." It is *seppun*. Yet, it is rarely heard. Instead, most young Japanese (those doing most of the kissing) use *kissu*, if they talk about it at all. It is felt that the use of English sanitizes by endistancing. The word becomes a euphemism. It is like (in all language) calling the toilet a hand-washing place. It indicates that though a word is somehow necessary, the designated action is not quite socially acceptable.

The reason that we in the West need not feel funny about kissing and that the Japanese do is that we have a much larger kissing repertoire. We have, as it were, domesticated the act.

We kiss just everyone. Mother, father, brother, sister, wife, children — no one is safe. The Japanese, however, still think of the kiss as an exotic adjunct to the act of making love. For a couple to kiss in public would be for them to publicly indulge in foreplay. And as for kissing Mom at train station or airport lobby, well. . . .

Thus the social role that kissing takes in Japan is narrow. It does not mean affection or reverence or sorrow or consolation or any of the other things it can mean in the West. It means just one thing and that is the reason for the ambivalence which surrounds it.

—1983

Pachinko

UNLIKE PINBALL, that restful, nearly horizontal game, *pachinko* is vertical, taller than the player, and noisy. While pinball indicates the score with flashing lights and a few bells, the sound of the moving balls itself softened with padded obstacles and rubbered baffles, pachinko is designed to be loud.

The name itself expresses the din. It is an onomatopoetic term imitative of the noisely racketing ball (*pachin*) and the clack it makes when it hits the bottom of the board (*ko*). The won balls (there is no score, winners simply receive more balls) swirl into the metal tray at the bottom with the roar of a molten torrent. There are often hundreds of machines within a pachinko parlor and there are over ten thousand such establishments within Japan. The sound is overwhelming. The balls fall vertically against the pins making a cascade of noise; the massed balls falling into the waiting tray created a cacophony.

In this aural inferno sit long lines of patrons, each before his own machine, oblivious of his neighbor. One thinks of the worst of the nineteenth-century factories, humans themselves half machine; the assembly line gone mad. Looking at the busy hands, the empty eyes, one also thinks of some kind of religious ceremony, something vaguely Tibetan with mandalas plainly visible and all the prayer-wheels whirling.

Yet, these people seem to be enjoying themselves. They have paid for the privilege of sitting there and working their levers. Many will thus sit for hours, intent, immune alike to discomfort and to din. Punishment, revelation — the joys of pachinko lie somewhere between the two.

The ostensible reward is material gain, that which seems to motivate all gamblers. The cost of 25 pachinko balls is only ¥100, same price as a pack of gum, less than a ride on the subway, much less than a pack of cigarettes. With these one has the chance of running up a fortune, it is said.

Certainly it seems to be with these hopes that all of the various techniques and expertise of the *pachipro,* the pachinko professional, is brought into play: finding the right parlor, the right machine; knowing when to start, when to quit; being able to tell at a glance the successful potential of one over the other.

Even so, one wonders if the winnings are commensurate with the various investments of time and money. In any event the massed balls are to be legally exchanged only for household goods (toothpaste, soap, towels, etc.) and for cigarettes. It is said that illegal money exchanges are also possible: you are given a marker and present yourself at some closed door at the end of a dark alley, knock, and get cash. Certainly popular is the semi-legal maneuvre of taking your soap and cigarettes to a small establishment next door which will relieve you of them at a price considerable less than if bought on the market.

Though the profit ability of pachinko in regards the patron is open to some doubt there is none at all regarding the propriator. Cultural commentator Rick Kennedy discovered that the total annual pachinko revenue is 7 trillion yen — this to be compared with, for example, the total value of all video tape recorders produced in Japan during 1986, which is only 3 trillion yen. Also that 20 percent of all cigarettes produced in Japan — not an inconsiderable number — are given away as pachinko prizes. For pachinko patrons then the attractions ought to be also other than economic.

In the West the charm of pinball is often social. A number of people lounge around the machine. Body English is observed and encouraging monosyllables are exchanged. The machine itself may be hit or otherwise encouraged. Light refreshments are often nearby and an atmosphere of relaxed play is achieved. Though individual pitted against machine may be occasionally observed, more usually a loose group is involved. And, in any event, the pinball hall has other attractions — the bar, many different kinds of playmachines, attractive strangers, and so on. The ambience is a relaxed one, friendly and sociable.

How different the pachinko hall. It contains nothing but row after row of standing machines. There is otherwise only the handbasin, the toilet, the pay telephone and the cashier's booth. There are no amenities, only necessities. Nor does one eat or drink or (because of the racket) talk; there is no soft lighting, only overhead glare; no innocuous mood music, only — occasionally heard above the clatter — the most spartan of wartime marches, played over and over again.

Here stand the hundreds, over Japan the millions, each sober in front of his machine, intent, earnest, feeding in the silver balls. There is no talk, no human sound at all. There is not even Body English (or Japanese) since the machines are not to be maltreated — they are equals, not servants. Serious, even dedicated, each person stands before his moving mandala. If it were not for the noise one might think of a church, so personal is each person's activity. Row upon row the patrons sit, as though in confessional booths.

The ambience is closed, solitary, even unfriendly. Pachinko is an intensely private occupation. There is nothing social about it.

Side by side, elbow by elbow, these people are, one might think, nevertheless in a kind of social situation. Perhaps, but there is no talk, no meeting of eyes, no indication from any one that he is other than alone. Even those who come in together are shortly lost to each other, each sitting solitary, each facing his own and, for the moment, private machine.

If winning itself is the object, winning not for the sake of goods nor money, but for its own abstract self, then either skill or luck should be the means. It seems, however, that neither are. There is no skillful way to catapult the clattering balls. Likewise, sheer luck, that happy combination of chance circumstances, seems unsought.

What is sought out is the proper machine. One of the mystiques of pachinko is that some machines are better than others and one must find one's proper mate. In this pursuit the player will initially try several machines until he locates one that feels right to him. This accomplished, he will remain faithful, unless disillusioned, in which case he will transfer his balls to another.

Veterans claim that the feel of a machine can be evaluated and appreciated after only a few tries. Others say they can just look and tell that somehow — as in falling in love — this one is the right one. As in the case with true love, however, unkind life creates many difficulties. Concerning this there is a whole body of folk belief.

The propriators tamper with the machines, to make them give more or less. Just before payday, for example, the machines are said to give more. It said that sudden rain after a hot spell can warp the back of the machines to the advantage of the players. Also, since bankrupt machines are so tagged by the management, it is best to arrive at those hours when these machines are restocked. Also there is the *kugishi* (or nail-"doctor") of whom to beware. This is a specialist called in to tilt certain pins in certain machines. This operation, which always occurs at night, prevents the rightness of a single machine from becoming notorious. Yesterday's winners will again repair to the right machine and find it wrong.

This belief in the ultimate rightness of certain machines lies in a faith that a slight tilt from the vertical will affect the performance. Seasoned players, believing this, try to counterweight their machines with loads of balls in the tray beneath. The perfect balance will, if the kugishi has not appeared overnight, result in a greater winning average.

But what is won? Not the goods — they are often cheaper outside. Not the prestige — no one is watching. Not a supposed skill nor an imagined luck. Something more is involved, since even the most successful locating of the right machine can not be considered an end in itself since no reward is involved.

The true purpose of the player would then seem to have little to do with the ostensible aim of his efforts. Though some have explained the attraction as constituting an articulated allegory of life itself — peculiar allegory, peculiar life — the answer would seem to lie in some less intellectual, some more spiritual direction.

An indication is that the game is addictive. One either plays pachinko a lot or one plays it very rarely if at all. There are to be sure occasional players waiting for a train or a late friend, but the majority are addicts. One goes to pachinko as one goes to the bottle. That millions thus addicted give rise to no national concern would indicate that the effects are found either benign or necessary.

In searching for a reason why anyone should become habituated to sitting in the cold or the heat, assailed by noise, watching thousands of balls fall through pins, and with no hope of even symbolic reward, one might look first into the origins of the game.

There was no pachinko in ordered, prewar Japan. It is a postwar development and sprang directly from defeat. Even before the ruined cities were fully reconstructed pachinko parlors had sprung up. The press referred to them as inexpensive places of pleasure, certainly innocently so in an otherwise pleasureless and poverty-stricken land. And even today there is an air of the immediate postwar era about these places: their often spartan if tawdry interiors, the bare necessities and nothing more, the long grey lines, the wartime marches. It was here that the thousands sought and found.

It was not pleasure they found, but oblivion. And this rewarded search has continued because the conditions which created it have continued. In the decades following the war, Japan has vastly improved in all ways except one. No substitute has ever been discovered for the emotional and spiritual certainty that this people enjoyed — almost alone in the world — until the summer of 1945.

A tightly-knit people, the largest single family in the world, Japan suffered an inner trauma, one which might be compared to that of the individual believer who suddenly finds himself an atheist. Japan lost its god, and the hole left by a vanished diety remains.

The loss was not the emperor, nor his sudden humanization. It was, however, everything which he and his whole ordered prewar empire stood for. It was certainty, no matter how disagreeable that certainty might become, that was lost. And this is something that the new postwar world did not replace. Indeed, the social fabric was even further rent. The individual, never allowed nor later taught any individual reliance, was eventually deprived of any real emotional kinship with country, with town or city, and finally with family. And all of this occurred in three decades — a change which traditional Japan could have accomplished in only three or more centuries.

The various pressures of city life are consequently very strongly felt in Japan, and pachinko is a big-city phenomenon — even now that every country crossroads has its parlor. It even first appeared in the grayest of all the industrial cities, Nagoya. Originally the patrons may have been the jobless and the hopeless. Now it is for those whose jobs are not enough. They repair to the pachinko parlor as others go to other places of addiction — bars, for example.

Like people in bars, those in the pachinko halls are feeling no pain. They are, rather, experiencing a kind of bliss. This is because they are in the pleasant state of being occupied, with none of the consequences of thinking about what they are doing or what any of it means. They have learned the art of turning off.

In this attainment boredom is requisite. Yet some activity — the droning of prayers or the monotone of machines, the telling of the beads or the clicking of the balls — is also necessary. The ritual may seem empty but it is not. It is filled with nothing. Oblivion is achieved.

Pachinko is thus, like all important distractions, only ostensibly about itself. Its true aim is far greater — this being nothing other than annihilation. The annihilation of self, a most pleasant state, may, for those successful, be indefinitely prolonged. Necessary for this is the location of the right machine, the one which seems to respond — the silent friend. This wordless communion between man and machine is just enough to offer an edge to oblivion, to keep the patron partially conscious of what he is doing, to keep him aware of his ostensible purpose in being there while, at the same time, gratefully surrendering his real reason. The pachinko parlor patron emerges refreshed, renewed.

One is reminded then of a religious exercise because the pachinko hall is, in its way, a kind of shrine or temple. One thinks of droning chants, and is reminded of *zazen* meditation, one of the aims of which is a liberation from the self through a stilling of that very self.

When one meditates one does not think. Expressly, the aim of meditation is to prevent the normal grazing pattern of the leashless mind. In meditation one is expected to curb the activities of this organ which is so solely responsible for any idea of self.

An aid to this is the ambiguous. The teacher may give the adept a seemingly meaningless riddle or *koan* to turn over and over in his mind. This keeps the brain busy but prevents its once more wandering through the rut-like patterns which it has established and which it calls self. Any answer to the riddle is arbitrary, but this arbitrary quality is not even recognizable until a degree of liberation from the mind and its ways has been achieved.

The pachinko machine may thus be seen as such an arbitrary object. One does not in any sense win with it. Rather, it occupies the attention and hence the mind. Both eyes and brain fastened to its noisy, shiny surface, the intelligence is blessedly stilled. Its enigmatic face merges with one's own. Lulled by the racket, fascinated by the glitter, one is alone, a community of singularity, and the familiar and contradictory self is allowed to rest.

Pachinko is in this way resembles not only drink, but also drugs, sex, fast driving, religion. It affords relief from self now that self, constricted, conscribed, yet denied both security and certainty, turns upon itself to create the state we call alienation. No wonder pachinko is habit-forming. It is respite.

That it is nothing more remains its limitation. Zazen begins only after the mind is properly stilled. Pachinko does nothing more after this stillness is properly accomplished. Zazen is a true medicine; pachinko, only a palliative.

Still, pachinko palace or pachinko barracks, the game has become an institution — like the public hospital. Pachinko therapy, offered at a most modest price, has never, of course, been openly recognized. The game is officially thought a harmless pastime and is ignored if not encouraged. And if you ask a player why he is there he always says that he is merely killing time.

Actually, he is killing much more than that. He is smothering the importunate and dissatisfied self. This he is doing — and again a Buddhist parallel is discernible — by living in the present moment, the instant now, his mind focused. He is calm, at rest and at peace. Cut off from the world by his magical machine, he regards the flow of the balls as saints are said to regard the ebb and tide of the world. The resulting illumination is not lasting but it is —as the continued and enormous popularity of pachinko indicates — better than none at all.

—1980

Walkman, *Manga* and Society

AMONG THE MOST successful new products in consumer-minded Japan is the Walkman. This device, for those few who may not know it, is a set of earphones wired to a portable radio and/or cassette-player. [While Panasonic, Sanyo, Nippon, Sony, and others manufacture versions of the cassette player, Sony's trade name "Walkman" has almost become the generic term for the device.]

As the name indicates, it is not to be used in the privacy of the home; it is to be used in public, specifically while walking, or at least moving.

Its benefits, according to the advertisements, include: putting one's time to good use by using foreign-language tapes; rendering one's journey agreeable by listening to music; informing and educating oneself by catching up with the latest news, cooking programs, etc.

The hype is thus toward both self-improvement and pleasure, and it is these positive elements of Walkman which are stressed by the manufacturers and by any user you may interrupt to ask.

Looking at the myriads of walkmen and walkwomen, however, a thought occurs. Is it not possible that the negative benefits are greater than the positive? Does not the true popularity of Walkman lie not in what it puts into the ears but what it keeps out?

The thought occurs for two reasons. First, I have never interrupted a language or cooking lesson. Rather, Walkman users are subjecting their ears to a very high-decibel combination of pop/rock/*enka*. Secondly, if my negative-input theory is correct, then Walkman constitutes a parallel to the uses to which another consumer item, the *manga*, is put.

Manga are enormously popular comic strip books in Japan. Dozens of weekly and monthly published titles are sold in hundreds of thousands of copies. Though the manga may be "read" in private, its public consumption is remarkable. Any train, any subway, any park bench is filled with those whose eyes are glued to their opened manga.

Here the hype stresses no self-improvement. Indeed with such success assured there is no need for manga advertisement. And in any event with a context so fatuous and complacent on one hand, so violent and salacious on the other, any suggestion of self-improvement would be ludicrous.

Instead, we are told that manga are entertaining. At least this is what I am told when I interrupt a reader's pleasure to ask. Manga are *omoshiroi* (interesting), I am informed. This is a palpable falsehood, no matter how sincerely voiced. One day, however, after much fruitless research and several direct snubs, when I was thus occupied in disturbing people, I received an answer that opened new depths. Manga, I was told, is a kind of portable television: it occupies, pleasantly enough, the brain while one is doing something else — sitting, standing, waiting.

The connection is made. Manga is to the eyes as Walkman is to the ears. Both are attractive for entirely negative reasons. Their salient quality is not input but, as it were, output. They both, like television, exclude.

And what is it that they so successfully exclude? Why, life itself. The others standing, sitting, squeezed; the urban crush and the urban clutter and clatter; rural emptiness, rural sprawl; an environment both packed and empty. The manga offers an absolutely inconsequential visual world which excludes and is preferred to the real one. The Walkman offers an aural world of equal inconsequentiality which veils both cacophony and stillness. Both Walkman and manga offer not only a substitute but also a secession.

The result is an alternate world, one which — given the popularity of both Walkman and manga — is preferred. One might say that users are audio-visual dropouts in that the aim of the devices is the exclusion of the real world. At the same time, however, such use is not only retreat. However pathetic, the results are that an attempt is being made to find a more habitable place.

One thinks of a parallel with the West — drugs. By comparison, Japan has only a minimal drug problem but the manga/Walkman effect does approximate the results of certain drug use: reality is in both cases veiled and, for addicts, the engendered false world is preferred. Another parallel, both manga and Walkman are addictive: the alternate "reality" is so much more pleasant. As with certain combinations of uppers and downers, a peaceful equilibrium is possible.

To say that Walkman and manga are only a fashion among the young answers no questions and seems to beg the one it suggests. Fashion is, by definition, the future. And, even in its most extreme manifestations it rises from need. Also, fashion is criticism — it can have meaning only when defined against an "unfashionable" status quo.

In the continuing popularity of Walkman and manga (and pachinko as well) it is possible to detect an implicit criticism. This can be seen as an answer by society to the activities of those who turned the country so madly consumerist, who wilfully ''developed'' nature to its present state of despoilation, and who have so thoroughly taught that the acquiring of wealth is the highest aspiration.

Not that the developers and the money-grubbers were not always within this society (and any other as well); rather, that in contemporary Japan these have come to assume greatest control. And there is but a thin difference between the man who (for aesthetic reasons) moves a rock a few centimeters this way, a bamboo grove a few centimeters that, and one who (for economic reasons) moves the rock entirely away and cuts down the bamboo grove. In both there is no respect for any original integrity. In both there is an insistance that the hand of man — specifically the hand of the Japanese man — forms. It is simply that the premises are different: in the landscape artist the aim is aesthetic gain; in the developer the aim is financial gain.

A form of criticism long favored in Japan is silence. One refuses to respond — the criticism is all the stronger for being unvoiced. One would like to believe this invisible criticism is there, right there: the Japanese younger generation — closed, eyes preoccupied, ears plugged, all senses sealed.

—1985